PRAISE FOR

Cooking Up a Business

"This book isn't just for anyone who is thinking about starting a food business; it's for anyone who is thinking about starting a business, period. These compelling profiles show that it's truly possible to make dreams a reality with hard work and the lessons gleaned from these entrepreneurs. My biggest takeaway? You get a lot of help and support from unlikely sources, including these intrepid souls who were willing to share their stories so that you can learn from their experiences."

—Michelle Shih, lifestyle director at *O, the Oprah Magazine*

"From flavored nut butters in Colorado to bargain wine in California, Rachel Hofstetter provides insight into an inspiring diversity of food businesses. Hofstetter's flair for storytelling illuminates these entrepreneurs' passion, dedication, and great success. *Cooking Up a Business* is a go-to for foodies with a taste for starting their own company, and a great reference for readers wondering how their favorite products got to the grocery store shelves."

—Leah Douglas, *Serious Eats*

"From local artisans to food tour enterprises, this terrific book shows a wide range of entrepreneurs pursuing their passions in food—and actually making a living! It's a valuable, instructive, and encouraging set of stories and practical advice—smart reading for anyone thinking of launching their own food endeavor."

—Faith Durand, executive editor of *The Kitchn*

"The specialty food industry is booming. Thousands of fledgling entrepreneurs want to bring their treasured recipes to market but are unaware of the obstacles they will encounter. This insider's look at successful businesses will instruct and inspire, so more people can live their dreams."

—Ron Tanner, vice president of communications and education at the Specialty Food Association

Cooking Up a BUSINESS

Lessons from Food Lovers Who Turned Their Passion into a Career—and How You Can, Too

Rachel Hofstetter

A PERIGEE BOOK

A PERIGEE BOOK
Published by the Penguin Group
Penguin Group (USA) LLC
375 Hudson Street, New York, New York 10014

USA • Canada • UK • Ireland • Australia • New Zealand • India • South Africa • China

penguin.com

A Penguin Random House Company

Library of Congress Cataloging-in-Publication Data

Hofstetter, Rachel.
Cooking up a business : lessons from food lovers who turned their passion into a career—and how you can, too / Rachel Hofstetter.— First edition.
pages cm
Includes index.
ISBN 978-0-399-16231-2
1. Cooking—Vocational guidance. 2. Food trade—Vocational guidance. 3. New products. 4. New business enterprises. I. Title.
TX652.4.H64 2013
641.30023—dc23 2013025940

First edition: December 2013

PRINTED IN THE UNITED STATES OF AMERICA

10 9 8 7 6 5 4 3 2

Text design by Tiffany Estreicher

To Kathleen, Steve, Tammy, and Lorne—
for giving me roots and wings.

CONTENTS

INTRODUCTION

So, You Want to Sell Your Famous Spaghetti Sauce?

You might call me a food entrepreneur groupie. At first it was for work: my job as a food editor at places like *O, the Oprah Magazine* and *Reader's Digest* took me to food trade shows, launch parties, and lots of meet-and-greets where I chatted with food entrepreneurs about their products. The chocolates, jams, cheeses, and crackers were delicious, but just as memorable were the founders' *stories*. When I went home at night, I wasn't thinking about their products per se, but the aha moments, challenges overcome, and sheer drive that had led each one from his or her home kitchen to bountiful displays on grocery store shelves.

It became one of my favorite parts of the job: A new food entrepreneur was in town next Tuesday. Did I want to meet? Of course! Or I'd give a friend a fantastic cheese to try and then spend twenty minutes waxing poetic about the story of the woman from Alabama who left her corporate job to raise goats and make fresh chèvre.

Then I found myself talking about the lessons I'd picked up to new and want-to-be entrepreneurs. It started small. My aunt had a special holiday herring dish and was thinking of selling it at her local market. How should she go about it? Advice came tumbling out—not from my own experience, but an amalgamation of the wisdom of the hundreds of food founders I'd worked with over the years. Then I'd be chatting with another food entrepreneur and he'd mention a challenge he was facing. Well, this other company had experienced something similar and overcome it by doing x, y, and z, maybe he could, too?

And thus this book was born. I wanted to focus on what it's like to start and grow a successful food business *now*, so I limited my net to entrepreneurs who had created their business in the past ten years or so. Pioneering food companies came out of the 1980s and 1990s, but what about those who came of age in an era of social media, Whole Foods, artisanal products, food trucks, blogs, and gluten-free? It's their stories that teach you how to succeed today.

I also wanted my dream list of food entrepreneurs to have founded their company and still be in control today; they had to be of all ages, genders, and life experiences; and I wanted to include businesses from all over the United States, from Columbus, Ohio, and Boulder, Colorado, to longtime foodie hotspots like San Francisco. These are the people who are just like *you*.

I think you'll agree that the final group—who will become your friends and mentors throughout these pages—are smart, savvy, and incredibly inspirational. Best of all, they're great teachers. For an entire year I conducted exclusive interviews with each entrepreneur, following along on his or her intrepid tales as we dove into both wins and mistakes. Often, I'd be swept away by the narrative, only to realize at the end that I'd learned more—intuitively—in one session than in any of the business lectures I'd taken in college.

I wanted their experiences to offer applicable, real-world guidance to the entrepreneur who is dreaming about the next big thing. Ten years ago, we couldn't have guessed that gluten-free crackers, salty savory chocolates, and popped potato chips would be runaway hits. And while I have no idea what yet-to-be-invented food products will be flying off shelves ten years from now, I do know that the down-to-earth, real-life lessons in this book will help the next generation of food entrepreneurs—*you*—get there.

You'll learn innovative ways to hustle so you can make and market your product on the cheap, get meetings with grocery store buyers, and build a national brand with no connections or start-up money, like the young couple who founded Love Grown Foods did. You'll learn from the found of Kopali Organics how to develop a product that sells, supports social good, and of course, returns profits. The best-friend cofounders at Tasty share how to create incredibly strong branding so that if your original product doesn't work out, you can easily navigate your way to the next iteration. And if a luxury brand is your goal, Katrina Markoff of Vosges is your woman—her high-end specialty chocolates are the food equivalent of couture fashion.

Join Phil Anson of Evol Foods as he navigates food safety regulations—everything from commercial kitchens to U.S. Department of Agriculture (USDA) inspections—and unearths the unique challenges of scale involved with selling fresh and frozen foods. The eponymous founder of Mary's Gone Crackers takes you on a wild ride through product manufacturing, including the world of co-packers and niche areas like gluten-free, and leaves you ready to bake, cook, bottle, or package anything.

You'll learn how to smartly use your biggest asset—equity in your company—to bring on and retain the best employees, hire premier design firms, and get your product into distribution. (You'll also be craving tour guide Justin Gold's nut butters.) Then you'll brush up on your business acumen with a genius approach to financing from Cameron Hughes Wine.

Once you're ready to launch and create big buzz, Keith Belling of Popchips will inspire you with his fresh, fun marketing and sampling campaigns. And then you can go really big like Kara Goldin of Hint Water, who explains how her keep-it-simple strategy makes her win on the grocery store shelf and why over half the stores in the United States are clamoring to carry her product.

Whew! It's enough to make you want to start cooking up a business. And when you do, drop me a line at rachel.hofstetter@gmail.com. I'd love to hear your delicious success story.

1

The Power of Hustle

LOVE GROWN FOODS

A young couple, fresh out of college, reinvents—and conquers—the cereal aisle.

A Love Story

Maddy D'Amato and Alex Hasulak first met briefly when they were freshmen at the University of Denver (he asked her to a dance—her answer will forever remain off the record). But it wasn't until two years later, when they were juniors, that they became more than casual acquaintances. "Then it was quickly a head-over-heels situation," remembers Maddy. "I saw Alex longboarding around campus, and it was nice to see someone I knew—most of my friends were studying abroad." She immediately texted him, and the next day they met for breakfast. Over a whirlwind of conversation they bonded over everything from early graduation (they were both planning on it) to their love of the outdoors.

When the check came, Alex instantly picked it up. If breakfast was on Alex, then Maddy was just going to have to cook him dinner to reciprocate. And when dinner was finished, the October night just happened to be full of shooting stars. Maddy and Alex made a thermos of hot cocoa, pulled on their coats, and drove to a lookout point with a view over all of Denver. "We lay out blankets and talked for hours, watching the stars until four in the morning. I would say we fell completely in love," remembers Maddy. Little did they know what would come from that late night adventure would be not just a relationship—but a thriving natural food business that, five years later, would have products in 4,500 stores.

Plan to Succeed, Succeed as Planned

It didn't take long for Alex and Maddy to become an official couple—and to share their emerging career dreams. Alex had dreamed of running his own business since his lemonade-stand days, while Maddy was an avid cook and nutrition guru. Was there a way to join forces and combine their passions? Within weeks, they were tossing ideas back and forth between every class. First, they considered selling Maddy's homemade pesto. But she and Alex were living in college houses—make that typical college houses, overflowing with roommates and with very limited fridge space. It would have been a logistical nightmare to store large amounts of basil and fresh pesto. Plus, after doing a few large test batches for friends, it was clear that while making pesto for six was a breeze, making it for sixty was exponentially more difficult.

That's when they both stepped back and looked not just at the company they wanted to run in six months, but the one they wanted in five years. Although they were brimming with enthusiasm and itching to start right away, Alex had also taken some business classes and knew

Mario Masitti

Maddy D'Amato and Alex Hasulak

that a little strategic planning on the front end would help them later—they would need to think small and local for the short term but plan for big and national in the long term. The first question to consider: What could he and Maddy eventually mass produce, while still maintaining high quality? If they began with something tricky now—like a perishable, high-labor product (pesto!)—they would run into issues as soon as they moved beyond a few area stores. Instead, they needed something that was shelf stable, easy to make and store in large batches, and simple to transport. In short, they needed a healthy food product that would scale.

And that's where Maddy's mother's granola came in. "My mom had made this recipe my entire life, and ironically, I'd never liked it. I love the memory of her making it and the smell, but it was never a food I liked to eat," says Maddy. But Alex loved her granola, and it had three big plusses going for it: it was nonperishable, transportable, and could be easily scaled for large batches. The couple took that recipe as a base and started tweaking it in their college kitchens, making all sorts of changes—one batch used honey, another used molasses; some tries were crunchy, some were chewy. Soon they had a variety of recipes they loved and were ready to pick a winner.

But before they could test their new product out on potential customers, they had to think of a name and a larger brand identity. That included brainstorming a list of thirty-plus possibilities while they were supposed to be studying for midterms. "My only request was that the name include *love* because I truly believe love makes everything taste better. It's the secret sauce," explains Maddy. They listed all sorts of phrases that had *love* as the first word—and the second Maddy wrote down *love grown*, it stuck.

But Love Grown granola was not their final goal: Love Grown Foods was. "We really envisioned ourselves growing into a natural foods company, not just a granola company," explains Alex. "We didn't want to limit ourselves with a name, in the same way we didn't want to limit ourselves with a product that wouldn't scale." In fact, they've never used the word *granola* on any packaging—their product is tagged Oat Clusters & LOVE. This also meant they could bypass any preconceived connotations of the word *granola* (think hippie, crunchy, counterculture).

Alex and Maddy also started to design their logo and began thinking about how they wanted to be perceived: fresh, happy, and most important, legitimate; no homespun vibe or amateur-looking packaging. From the beginning, Alex had a "building-a-brand mentality," focusing on that intangible value that's more than just a product. The branding was integral to how they wanted to grow. "Think of how something goes viral on the Internet," says Alex. "It needs exponential growth."

What does someone love and then tell ten friends about? And then those ten friends tell another ten friends? It's generally fun, optimistic, and appealing to a large—not niche—audience. A cute, premium-priced product in a boutique Denver coffeehouse can go only so far in sales and impact. But an optimistic brand, tied to a delicious, accessible, and competitively priced product? The potential was exponential.

Once they had a name and the beginnings of a brand, Alex and Maddy took a cue from business textbooks: If the big companies put new products through exhaustive customer focus group research, so would they. But they didn't need to hire expensive consultants when they had hundreds of college classmates who loved free food. Alex and Maddy filled snack-size plastic bags with samples, printed Love Grown Foods on return address labels, and stuck them on. Then they attended every one of their classes laden down with samples for their peers and professors: The only caveat was that anyone who tried the oat clusters had to fill out a short survey. Did they like it crunchy or soft? Extra sweet or just subtly sweet? What flavors did they prefer? Would they buy it at a store? How much would they be willing to pay? What did the name and logo communicate? Their first, grassroots attempt at focus groups and consumer research was a hit: "We took every bit of feedback into consideration and used it to refine our recipe, product line, and vision," says Maddy. "And in those last few weeks before graduation, we began to get a better idea of exactly what our company should be."

Success, One Step at a Time

After graduating in May 2008, the couple moved in with Maddy's parents, a special education teacher and a contractor, in Aspen, Colorado. Alex never even considered renting their own place; he wanted to save as much money as possible so he and Maddy could launch their business. "It took me a while to get on board with that!" remembers Maddy. While she enjoyed working on Love Grown, she still thought of it as a side project, something to keep Alex occupied while she earned certifications in massage therapy, Pilates, and nutritional counseling. And on the surface, that's all it looked like: Alex was working full-time as a teller at the Wells Fargo bank; Maddy was using her new certifications to land a variety of part-time jobs. Plus, three nights a week they'd go straight from their long days to a joint babysitting job. But throughout late 2008 and early 2009, they were also putting Google to work, figuring out all of the steps of manufacturing and packaging their product.

Alex was adamant that the product be fully branded and "real" looking the first time it saw retail shelves, so each exercise took extra time and deliberation. Although it would cost more upfront—which Alex and Maddy compensated for by putting in extra manual labor—their hope was that this strategy would make it easier for their company to grow and scale. For example, they could have originally put the product into plastic bags and sold them in Aspen coffee shops, but then the granola would scream, "Homemade!" Because custom-printed bags were prohibitively expensive, Alex and Maddy came up with a cheaper solution: they ordered large printed stickers as well as clear, sturdy stand-up bags. "We'd hand sticker our bags for hours and hours," says Maddy. "We'd put on a movie and it became our hang-out time." With a little creativity and extra work, they soon had Love Grown bags that would fit in on any supermarket shelf.

They also had to tackle barcodes and nutrition labels. Time and again, Alex returned to Google to find his answers. It turns out that there's actually only one company that issues Universal Product Code

(UPC) barcodes, GS1 (gs1us.org). The cost can add up quickly—$1,000 to register your company and then an additional fee to generate the barcodes for your packaging. And those barcode fees are per item, so if you have five flavors, you're buying a specific UPC for each one. But once they were done with that, they were done—every retail store in the world uses the same standard GS1 barcoding system, and there are no per-swipe fees or extra charges.

To get their official nutritional information, Alex and Maddy skipped the traditional route (hire a company to run analysis) and did a little bit of digging. They found that Colorado State University, like many other universities, would run reduced-price tests for small businesses. Soon they had all the documentation they needed to create a nutrition label, and their packaging prototype was looking more and more like the big-name products they saw in grocery stores. Then it was all about registration, taxes, and health regulations. "Besides Google, I think the best resources for all things official, like regulations, are government sites like sba.gov [Small Business Administration]," says Alex. "It can be like reading a foreign language, but at least you don't have to take it with a large grain of salt like you do on third-party websites."

By the spring of 2009, Alex and Maddy were finally ready to make some food! They rented space in a commercial kitchen from a catering company and bought huge bags of ingredients at Costco. The kitchen was in a basement, so they would haul hundreds of pounds of oats, honey, and oil down steep steps. They baked at night (the catering company used the space during the day), packaging and hauling their product back up the stairs before dawn.

Alex and Maddy started by bringing their oat clusters to two local coffee shops, small places that readily agreed to put the granola on their shelves because Maddy had known the owners most of her life.

But even at this stage, pricing was strategic. "Our hope was to eventually compete with the Bear Nakeds of the world," explains Alex. "We were never going to be able to do that with a retail price of $8.99, which puts you in a niche, luxury category." So he checked out the Bear Naked price, which was about $4.99, at various stores and decided that Love Grown would match it—even if it meant that, in the beginning, they weren't making enough to cover their costs.

Meanwhile, Alex was still working at Wells Fargo by day. A few times each week, the manager of the Aspen City Market grocery store would come in with cash deposits. "It was a small town, and so I knew who this guy John was, and by then he knew my name too," says Alex. So one day he just asked John for advice: "My girlfriend and I own a natural food company, and we would love to know what it takes to eventually get on your shelves." "Bring it in! Let me look at it," was John's enthusiastic reply.

They found that the support network in a small town, especially when you know lots of people like Maddy did in Aspen, is an amazing base. The outreach works in concentric circles: start with the people you know, then build a following in a bigger circle, and then an even bigger circle. But if you start in a big circle (say, Denver as opposed to Aspen), you don't have that same level of organic support. In Alex's case, John was just a nice guy he knew, so it was easy to casually ask for advice. But that one small connection would lead Alex and Maddy to their next concentric circle.

Two days later, Alex and Maddy took their fully branded bags of oat clusters into the store and showed them to John. "This is great!" he said. "I'll put it on the shelves in July." That was just a month and a half later, and two jaws dropped in tandem. How were they going to make that much product? But they rallied, baked up hundreds of bags' worth, and delivered it down the street. "And it just sold like crazy—it far outsold the leading, established store brands on the shelf," says Maddy. "We attribute that partially to the fact that I grew up in Aspen and we had incredible support from all of the locals. But at the same time, it was also a testament to the fact that people actually really liked the product because they didn't just buy it once, they kept on buying it."

Their success was so unprecedented that by the end of the first month, John told the couple that they needed to talk to King Soopers, a larger chain of grocery stores in the Denver area. "This is a product I can see going places," he said. He helped arrange a meeting, and in August 2009, Alex and Maddy packed up samples, drove down to Denver, and presented the product to the regional King Soopers buyers.

"The most difficult part of a meeting like that is actually *getting* the meeting, which was where we were very fortunate," says Alex. "Our success in Aspen obviously led to that invitation. There's no way a mom-and-pop company can walk in from the street to the offices of a conventional grocery chain and present their product. But we had the branding, the packaging, and the right price point, plus help from John."

But for the meeting itself, they knew the best thing they could bring was their own energy and passion. "Maddy naturally connects with people, which we learned helps us out a lot in presentations," explains Alex. "I know I'm biased, but she's an incredible salesperson." And while they made (and continue to make) PowerPoint presentations, they don't practice what they'll say or rely on their slides. "We live this business, so I hope we know what we're talking about!" says Alex, laughing. "We just go in there and talk about the product and our passion for healthy eating."

Soon King Soopers came back with unbelievable news: They were

Mario Masitti

The Love Grown line

going to carry Love Grown oat clusters in forty stores throughout the state. The Love Grown duo was ecstatic, but also needed to move quickly. The first order would start in January—just a couple of months away—and they needed to figure out how to juggle this new big order with their regular full-time jobs. Up until that point, Love Grown Foods had truly been a project they ran on the side. But even with forty stores, they could still handle baking at night, right? Halfway through their planning, King Soopers called again: Actually, they didn't want to place the product in forty stores. They wanted to put it in eighty.

From Zero to Sixty in Nine Months

The second King Soopers request came at the beginning of December, and the product would need to go on shelves in early January. Suddenly, Maddy and Alex had a lot to work out, and quickly. They took the risk, quit their jobs, found commercial kitchen space in Denver, and found a Denver roommate: Maddy's brother. They moved in all of their baking supplies and started to make their oat clusters during the last week of December, just like they'd made it hundreds of times before.

But unfortunately, the kitchen's ovens weren't baking evenly, and they couldn't get the product to come out right. "It was the most traumatic experience! We actually hauled our ingredients four hours back to Aspen," remembers Maddy, "and baked our first big order in our old commercial kitchen." They did the whole thing in twenty-four hours straight. Maddy's parents and brother came in to help bag, and no one stopped, or took a single break, for the whole stint. At the end of their nutty adventure, they repacked their car with bags of oat clusters and zoomed back to Denver. They were going to make their first deadline, and King Soopers would never know how heroic the attempt had been.

And so began the nine months of their lives that Maddy still refers to as "Brutal. Really, really brutal." The duo worked out the oven situation and started a daily routine of baking from 4 p.m. to 4 a.m., the window they'd purchased at the commercial kitchen. With no machines or industrial mixers—not even a KitchenAid!—they would literally hand-mix hundreds of pounds of ingredients at a time. "It was *hard*, physically demanding baking—we called it the granola workout—and it definitely kept us in shape," says Maddy. And when the going got tough, they'd remember the competitive athletes they'd been in high school and channel that power, giving each other pep talks reminiscent of a football coach's halftime talk: "Okay, finish strong. You have two more hours. Pull it together, and finish strong!"

They would even smell like granola long after they left the kitchen: Maddy recalls the scent of cinnamon seeping out of her pores in the shower. Alex and Maddy kept the intense schedule up night after night, week after week—and there was no falling into bed at 7 a.m.!

After a quick shower and change of clothes, they'd leave the house at the break of dawn to do a breakfast surprise for a store account or drop off oat clusters and yogurt at a morning radio show. Their strategy: Try everything possible in hopes of getting people talking about—and recognizing, and buying—Love Grown oat clusters.

During the day they were out and about: at farmers' markets, races, concerts, and in-store demos, all in the name of facilitating one-on-one engagement. By early evening, they'd be back baking in the kitchen. "Sleep? Who needs sleep?" says Maddy. "We were pulling twenty-four-hour shifts on a such a regular basis that it became our idea of normal."

It almost makes Alex sick to remember those early days now: "Those first nine months in Denver were like nothing else; it was extremely rough. I'll meet people today, and they think we just went on a joyride and got lucky. But no: it was a constant, never-ending sacrifice." They didn't have weekends, time off, or a cent of disposable income. In fact, they didn't have a single purely social interaction for nine months straight.

But the pair had no other options: They couldn't afford to bring anyone else on. There was no money to hire bakers or outsource to a co-packer or find people to do demos. "All we could afford was our own sweat and hard work!" says Maddy. "If we wanted something to get done, we had to do it." Their biggest relief? Sometimes, when they got big orders, they'd call on their parents for help and the whole crew would pull a marathon baking and packaging session.

While Alex and Maddy passionately believed in their company, others were skeptical. "Oh, that's cute, but you guys are twenty and twenty-one . . . you'll grow up and get real jobs soon," they'd hear, over and over. But the laughter and dismissals simply fueled their fire. They knew they had no baking experience, no work experience, and no business experience. What they did have was youth, energy, and nothing to lose. There were no responsibilities like kids or mortgages to color their perception of risk. "For us, this *was* the ideal time to attempt this," says Alex. "Not later, when we had years of experience and equity and people to take care of—now."

And all the while, they funded almost every step of their initial expansion themselves (they eventually took on a $10,000 loan from family to purchase a larger oven). How did they make it work? They'd managed to save almost every penny they made in 2008, among their five jobs each, and that's what they turned to now. To stretch those pennies further, everything they did—like baking batches of granola themselves in the middle of the night—was lean and cheap. This wasn't investors' "free" money they were spending, it was the hourly wages they'd earned one babysitting gig at a time.

So Maddy and Alex went all in together, saying, "We're either going to make it or we won't," and poured everything they had into the business. "We ask ourselves a lot, Is it worth the sacrifice? At the end of the day, we believe it always is," says Alex. "I have this philosophy: I will happily dedicate everything I have to this for five years. But on the first day of that sixth year, I'm going to look around and hope that my dreams and plans have come true—and that's when I'll allow myself to be elated."

Replicating the "Maddy Magic"

In the midst of all these delirious hours and backbreaking work, a crucial question remains: How on earth did Alex and Maddy bring a new product into an already oversaturated granola and cereal market? And not only a saturated market but a big-brand, big-money saturated market (think of Kellogg's, Post, and General Mills and the millions of dollars they put behind their brands). "Pure and simple, it was Maddy," says Alex. "Sure, we hustled and planned for the long term. But at the end of the day, Maddy was the best salesperson anyone had ever met. It's some combination of passion and enthusiasm and speaking from the heart."

How did Maddy—who was still only twenty-two at the time—become such a phenomenal salesperson? She started from a place of genuine conviction. "My ultimate goal is to get people thinking about whole grains and minimally processed, real food, even if they don't buy Love Grown," she explains. "I truly believe that there needs to be a change in the food system. A majority of the diseases in America are preventable with lifestyle changes, but there's a disconnect. People know it, but they don't act on it." When she and Alex do product demos in King Soopers, they see families fill their carts up with junk food with nary a vegetable in sight. "It's heartbreaking—young kids munch on a whole bag of chips as their moms shop," says Maddy. She was originally taken aback, especially because Colorado was supposed to be the healthiest and trimmest state in the Union. But Maddy thought that Love Grown—with its simple, short ingredient list, focus on whole grains, and affordable price—could help turn the tide. To do that, she started spending a good portion of her time speaking in elementary schools, becoming an effervescent cheerleader for healthy eating. "You can't sell something you don't believe in," she says. "So find something you believe in, create a product that backs it up, and then tell your story."

Sell, Design, and Build

Regardless of their big ideals and mission, Maddy and Alex couldn't just *tell* store buyers, media, and especially potential customers about how delicious and important their whole grain granola was; they had to *show* them. And show them they did, producing thousands upon thousands of single-serve samples that they would give away with wild abandon. "The idea of giving away your product—for free!—is one of the hardest things to wrap your head around as a start-up," says Maddy. "Because you see every sample as a dollar sign: 'That bag cost me $5.' You're so attached to every single product you make because it came from all of your blood, sweat, and tears."

Granola is, and was, a complicated and competitive supermarket category. To create Love Grown brand recognition and affinity, Alex and Maddy had to convince themselves that the best thing they could do was let people try their product—to have them put it in their mouths and taste it. "Putting a great product on the shelf wasn't enough if no one ever took it off the shelf," says Alex. "Even if we didn't see an immediate payoff, we forced ourselves to give out more and more product."

The pair emphasized just getting samples out there, rather than on detailed tracking of their marketing attempts. Whenever they thought they needed more, they whipped it up, a philosophy that's part of their general operating strategy: sell, design, and build. "We don't necessarily design our plan first, and then sell it, and then build and deliver," explains Alex. When King Soopers gave them eighty stores, they could have easily said, "Nope. We can't do that. That's not part of the plan." Instead, their reaction was "All righty! Now we're going to

"HUSTLE" AS A MISSION STATEMENT: BACK TO THE ROOTS

During their last semester as undergrads at the University of California at Berkeley, friends Nikhil (Nik) Arora and Alex Velez came up with a crazy idea to hold off the coming era of the real world: Could they raise gourmet mushrooms at home? Today, their grow-your-own-mushroom kits (which feature used coffee grounds from Peet's Coffee & Tea as the "soil") are sold in almost every Whole Foods, Home Depot, Nordstrom, Safeway, and Bed Bath & Beyond in the country. The secret to their seemingly overnight success, they say, is summed up by the first word in their mission statement: *Hustle.*

Here's how they've put their hustle to work at Back to the Roots:

1. Take your product to the top. Nik and Alex were college seniors when they first started playing with the idea of growing mushrooms in used coffee grounds—a concept a professor had mentioned in a biology class. Before they left for spring break, they planted mushroom spores in ten old paint buckets and left them on the floor of Alex's fraternity house. When they returned a week later, one of the buckets was sprouting mushrooms. In their excitement, Nik and Alex immediately took their mushrooms—bucket and all—to the best restaurant they could think of, the local Chez Panisse. Owner and food visionary Alice Waters happened to be there and was intrigued. She asked her chef to sauté up a few of these ultra-local, sustainable mushrooms. They were delicious, and Alice became their very first fan.

Then Nik and Alex picked up their mushroom bucket and continued walking down the street to the Berkeley Whole Foods. "The very first official store employee we saw was a guy stocking vegetables," says Nik. "So we excitedly showed him our bucket and told him our story. Customers gathered around, and the Whole Foods manager came over to see what the commotion was. He gave us the email address of his supervisor, and asked us to reach out." And the rest, as they say, is history.

2. Never, ever sit down. "When we first started exhibiting at trade shows—where a booth costs at least $4,000!—we were amazed that so many exhibitors would sit behind their booths, looking bored and just waiting for someone to come up and talk to them," says Nik. "We quickly made a rule for our team: Never, ever sit or stand behind the table. Always be in front of it, out in the aisles, energetic and in people's faces. We can't afford to sit quietly! We should be exhausted by the end of the show, and our neighbors should either be mad at us for attracting all the attention, or coming over to learn how we did it."

3. Need an answer? Plug and chug until you find a solution. When Nik and Alex were trying to get their kits in front of Home Depot buyers, they kept coming up against one closed door after another. "It was a veritable labyrinth, and we couldn't get any information," remembers Nik. So one day he walked into his local Home Depot and asked to speak to the manager. Without giving anyone time to think, he asked the manager for the name of *his* manager—that was it. He didn't ask for contact information or a referral request, or anything that would cue the manager's natural instinct to say no. The name was blurted out, and Nik walked off, happy.

At home, he wrote an email to the regional manager. He then sent it out, in email after email, to every possible iteration of the manager's name: Joe.Schmoe. JoeSchmoe. JSchmoe. On and on, until Nik had come up with more than twenty variations, each paired with possible Home Depot domains. And of all the emails he sent, one went through to the right person. "Sure, Home Depot might be interested," came the reply. "Could you meet in San Diego tomorrow?" And just like that, Nik and Alex hopped on a plane and landed their first Home Depot account.

figure out how to design and build that." The same idea worked with their sampling techniques; they were going to give away as much as possible—selling the brand, if not yet actual product—and then design and build their infrastructure as needed.

And in September 2010, nine months after Alex and Maddy had moved to Denver and started their exhausting journey, their punishing schedule began to pay off. Their first big break had been getting into the Aspen City Market—one store. Their second big break had been getting into the Colorado King Soopers—eighty stores. And their third big break would mean just the type of exponential growth Alex had dreamed of when he and Maddy first started brainstorming two years earlier.

Exponential Success

City Market and King Soopers are part of Kroger, a large supermarket corporation that operates almost two dozen chains of grocery stores across the country, including Fred Meyer, Ralphs, Smith's, and of course, the namesake Kroger. Love Grown Foods was doing well in King Soopers when Alex and Maddy were given the opportunity to present to Kroger. The meeting was a reflection of the support they were receiving from the King Soopers management, who unequivocally said, "Yes. We believe in this product." "Without that, we would never, ever have gotten our meeting with Kroger," explains Maddy.

But a meeting, they knew, was no guarantee of a buy. A number of industry people warned Alex and Maddy to keep their expectations in check—unlike Whole Foods, Kroger wasn't known for pioneering young companies. On a crisp fall day in September 2010, Alex and Maddy stepped off a plane in Cincinnati, Ohio, and headed to the only car company that would rent to them (for double the normal rate) because they were still under twenty-five. "It put our age in perspective, that's for sure," says Maddy. "We would have to make extra sure to come off as professional and confident in our abilities." The next morning, they showed up for their meeting in suits, polished from head to toe. And they went big: Alex and Maddy pitched that they would take as many stores as Kroger would give them. "It was our philosophy of sell, design, build," says Alex. "If they wanted our oat clusters, we knew we'd figure out how to make it happen." They left the meeting knowing they'd tried their best—and with no idea of whether their best was abysmal, good, or great.

Two months later, Kroger called: They were going to launch Love Grown in 750 stores, and take four of their five flavors. "You can imagine how far our jaws dropped *this* time!" says Maddy. And within minutes, they started to design and build. They knew it was finally time to raise capital, find a facility where they could manufacture the oat clusters full-time, and hire employees. They brought on a chief operating officer, found a team to start manufacturing the product, and ramped up production.

Two weeks into the process, they got another call from Kroger. The request was strangely familiar to their King Soopers experience: "Actually . . . we're not going to launch you into 750 stores." Pause. "We're launching you into 1,300."

"And that," says Maddy, "was when our jaws *fully* hit the ground. We were ecstatic, which really shows that we were naive and fearless." While an experienced businessperson might have preferred to establish themselves in the 750 stores first and then scale up, Maddy and Alex simply said yes and ran with it.

This was to be Love Grown's tipping point, when all of their early attention to scaling became necessary. Because of the conscientious steps they'd taken over the years—choosing a shelf-stable product, setting up professional-looking packaging, following all national regulation guidelines—they could now quickly expand. Alex and Maddy moved into their own facility in Denver, including a warehouse in which to stack pallet upon pallet of raw ingredients: 2,000-pound bags of oats, vats of honey, and sacks of nuts and dried fruits. They needed 50,000 bags for their first order, almost *seven times* what they were making just a month earlier. In a few short weeks, they scaled up tremendously and were running two shifts of production a day, five days a week. In January 2011—just eighteen months after Alex and Maddy had put their first granola bags on the shelf in Aspen—they sent off the Love Grown destined for 1,300 Krogers.

It Takes a Team

These days, Alex and Maddy aren't letting the flush of success slow them down. They're launching new product lines (the first out is oatmeal) and are continuing to grow their reach and promote the brand. And through it all, they're in it together. "I have to admit that the only way we're able to do what we do—we're at the office or out promoting the brand fourteen hours a day, seven days a week—is because we're doing it right next to each other," says Maddy. "I think about how lonely those long hours would be if just one of us were running this business. But Alex is my best friend, and to work with him every single day and build something together that we both care so much about . . . I really believe that's one reason we've been so successful."

For Alex, working with Maddy is one of the reasons he loves waking up every day and coming to work. The other reason is pure entrepreneurial thrill: "All of the blood, sweat, and tears we put into this have now come back as benefits in one way or another," he says. "And it's not just monetary benefits, but having real ownership in our business and being able to make big decisions on a daily basis." By 2013, only four years into operation, Love Grown Foods oat clusters were sold in over 4,500 stores—and Alex and Maddy were just celebrating their twenty-sixth and twenty-seventh birthdays.

TAKE AWAY

- **If you're not rolling in dough, hustle your way to success.** Find cheaper, grassroots alternatives for things like branding, packaging, UPC barcodes (gs1us.org), nutrition labels (go to a local university), market research (find hungry subjects, like college classmates, who will try and offer feedback on your product for free), and ingredients. (Hello, Costco!) And take a free hint from the business textbooks and think of the long term: What can scale?

- **Sell first, then design and build.** Go over the top and give away as much product as you can, and say yes to anything you possibly can. Convince stores that they want to carry your product, and then design and build infrastructure as needed once they say yes.

- **Start local.** If you can build a track record of success at a small, local grocery store that's affiliated with a larger chain, you up the chances of finding advocates who can help open doors to larger things. Go where you know you'll have success, hustle like crazy, and then build outward.

2

Designing a Sellable, Profitable Product

KOPALI ORGANICS

Zak Zaidman, a former technology entrepreneur, is on a mission: Better the lives of small family farmers around the world by selling humanely produced organic chocolate in the United States.

The Social Entrepreneur

Zak Zaidman's enthusiasm hits you immediately. "Seriously," he says, holding up a small bag of chocolate-covered espresso beans and shaking it. "This little treat can change the world." The forty-five-year-old, who was raised in Mexico City and today resides outside Los Angeles, sports a practical brown backpack filled with chocolate and Fair Trade literature in lieu of a traditional briefcase. It may seem that the self-described "relentless optimist" was destined to be a save-the-world type, but Zak didn't start out pursuing a career in food or social justice; his story begins in the heady world of dot-com technology start-ups. When Zak sold his virtual reality company in 2001, he decided to stay on, leading feel-good programs like rope courses and meditation sessions.

It was what happened after those meditation sessions that got Zak thinking. His coworkers—some of the technology industry's top developers, designers, and businesspeople—would chat, and invariably, the topic would shift to a lingering sense of dissatisfaction with their jobs. Instead of creating yet another website or software system, wasn't there something *real* they should be doing? Zak dreamed about turning those brilliant, interdisciplinary people loose on some social or environmental problem. Could they solve it using their business know-how?

Of course, Zak wasn't the first to arrive at the idea that business could be harnessed to promote social good. Environmentalists like Paul Hawken have long advocated measuring success not just by financial profit, but by the positive return to society (today, the concept is widely referred to as *social enterprise*). And while Zak's proposals didn't gain leverage in his Silicon Valley days, he had found the guiding philosophy that would propel him toward starting Kopali Organics.

When Life Takes You to Costa Rica . . .

"Stephen, I'm getting divorced," Zak typed two years later, his words racing 3,000 miles south to a remote outpost in Costa Rica. He'd been married for just six months, and he was the first to describe it as an explosive failed attempt. Stephen Brooks, Zak's longtime friend, wrote back immediately: "Thank God you're out of that hell. Come to Costa Rica."

Years earlier Stephen had founded a center for sustainable living in

Stephen Brooks

Zak Zaidman in Punta Mona

Costa Rica, a place called Punta Mona on a slip of land between the warm Caribbean Sea and the vibrant rain forest. He was growing his own food, working closely with the indigenous farmers, and teaching groups of visiting American high schoolers. And as the painful months rolled by, Zak felt himself healing in this landscape where the sun set each night in a bright haze of orange, and the ultra-floral scent of ylang-ylang trees lingered. "I thought I'd stay there for the rest of my life," says Zak. "It was pure, healthy, and above all, I loved the absolute connection to the land and ecosystems. Paradise? I thought I'd found it."

But soon after, Stephen told Zak a story. He was driving through the local indigenous area of Bribri when the jungle opened up to an ocean of yellow bananas stretching for miles. "I heard a deafening noise overhead, and I was sure I was witnessing a plane crash; there was the plane, just a hundred yards above me, spewing smoke into the air. It was going to fall any second; my heart stopped. And then the realization struck: the smoke was fungicide, being sprayed with wild abandon over the surrounding banana crops. My eyes burned, my throat clogged, and I quickly rolled up my windows and peeled out of there.

"And then I noticed the playground, full of kids playing soccer. I was racing to get away so I wouldn't have to breathe a drop of the poison, and this was their daily life."

Zak soon experienced the same thing again and again as he roamed the area more on his own. "The planes would drop literal tons of pollution over banana plantations every day. I met the men who were infertile, the farmers with cancer," he says. "And yet billions of these perfectly yellow bananas were being shipped around the world, to fill cereal breakfast bowls with fruit for nineteen cents a pop. We, as Americans, were sponsoring generations of cancer in places like Costa Rica each morning when we sliced our bananas—and we just didn't know."

From Problem to Product

Zak's social enterprise philosophy finally had a problem to solve. What could the Costa Rican farmers grow and make—organically, so they could have a humane quality of life—that could be sold in the United States? It would have to be a product with enough value added to monetarily support the farmers, which meant commodities like plain bananas were out.

Zak was able to realistically consider such a venture only because of earlier social enterprise initiatives that had organized many of the area's independent, subsistence organic farmers into cooperatives. These groups had streamlined their logistics and had already gained organic certification, but they needed more and bigger markets for their products. The idea was to take what these small organic farmers already did and act like a "gallery" for their "art": Zak and Stephen would market the product for a U.S. audience and promote the farmer's true stories.

After lots of conversations with community members, they had their genius product idea: organic banana vinegar. Never heard of it? Neither had any of their gourmand, food-loving friends back in the states, which meant that there would be no competition for such a unique item. The vinegar itself tasted like a cross between tangy apple cider vinegar and sweet, ripe bananas. It was used in countless local dishes, but was completely undiscovered outside of the Caribbean. Better yet, it was a nonperishable, value-added product that farmers could make without any high-tech capital expenditures—all that's needed are peeled bananas and wooden barrels. "It sounded like the perfect thing to introduce to the United States," says Zak. "And at the same time, our friends would have a market for their organic bananas."

Over the next few months, Zak and Stephen figured out how to design and manufacture their first bottles of banana vinegar. They also cast a wider net to increase their chances of successfully convincing a retailer to stock their yet-to-be-named concept. They sourced organic dried fruits, jams, coconut oil, and chocolate products from small co-operatives throughout Costa Rica. Then they practiced their pitches, took photographs of the pesticide-laden fields, and packed their bags full of the vinegar and other exotic treats. They set their sights on Los Angeles and the 2005 Lifestyles of Health and Sustainability (LOHAS) conference, which gathers entrepreneurs who focus on health, fitness, the environment, personal development, sustainable living, and social justice. The conference would be full of people who shared Zak and Stephen's ideals, but there was one person in particular they wanted to connect with: Michael Besancon.

Besancon became a pioneer in the industry in the 1970s, when he opened one of the first natural foods stores in the United States. He'd moved on to become president of the Whole Foods South Pacific region, which included Los Angeles, Phoenix, and Las Vegas. When Zak and Stephen tracked him down at the conference and finagled a few minutes of his time, Besancon listened. They told him their story and pulled out an abundance of pictures of the farmers, planes dropping pesticides, whole families plagued with health problems, the organic farm at Punta Mona, and small organic cooperatives that just needed a market for their products. By the time they were done talking, Besancon was enamored. Zak and Stephen weren't typical businessmen, trying to eke out a profit—they were two passionate guys trying to help their friends and neighbors.

"Will our business completely solve all of these problems?" Zak asked Besancon rhetorically, as Stephen pulled the banana vinegar and an array of other exotic treats out of his bag like a magician. "No. It's not a black-and-white issue. However, these small, indigenous farmers around the world live sustainably and harmoniously, but they're struggling to survive. They can't compete with the cheap food grown by the multinational, large-scale, chemically intensive companies. We can change that; we can support and value the work they do."

This deep, all-encompassing belief was Zak and Stephen's unique—and ultimately successful—strategy. "We weren't simply trying to sell a delicious product; we were inviting people to join us in creating something important," explains Zak. Here was a modern-day, good-for-all version of Robin Hood. Who wanted to join? Whole Foods said yes with a game-changing $100,000 buy. They wanted everything: banana vinegar, coconut oil, dried fruits, chocolate. While the game was far, far from over, Zak and Stephen now had a ticket to play.

Kopali, Take One

Zak and Stephen were ecstatic, but there was no time to celebrate: The next challenge surfaced almost immediately. There weren't enough organic farmers and suppliers in Costa Rica to provide the amounts Whole Foods wanted, so they suddenly needed to look beyond their own local network. Zak considered his Mexican roots and realized that the kind of organic scale they needed was building there. He and Stephen soon found a group in Mexico with similar motivations: to provide a living wage and sustainable community infrastructure for indigenous farmers. They had their own line of products and had already figured out the supply chain, from sourcing to packaging.

Zak appreciated that supply chain, because he'd gone through the exhausting process for the banana vinegar production himself. He'd tracked down each necessity piece by piece: First he sourced the bottles, then he found a bottling company in the Costa Rican capital of San José. They agreed to take the vinegar in fifty-five-gallon drums and pasteurize it, bottle it, label it, and pack it in cases. The bottling company was big enough that they knew how to export and navigate U.S. Food and Drug Administration (FDA) regulations but small enough to take a meeting with a small, unknown brand. "Each and every step was a substantial project!" says Zak. If this group in Mexico had already figured it out, he and Stephen were more than willing to build on their infrastructure.

Zak and Stephen wanted to include every delicious thing they tried in their line—after all, they were in an exploratory prototype phase. "We had more products than you could ever support properly or intelligently as a brand," explains Zak. "If we found a food that seemed unique, we added it. Something was bound to stick. We just didn't know what it was yet."

Take, for example, the vinegar. "It's not like we were inventing vinegar," says Zak. "But we told ourselves the kinds of stories you have to tell yourself as an entrepreneur. Like, thirty years ago, no one in America had ever heard of balsamic vinegar and now everyone has a bottle. We can do the same with banana vinegar!" In *The United States of Arugula*, David Kamp shares the compelling entrepreneurial story of how exotic balsamic vinegar became mainstream: Giorgio DeLuca, co-owner of the specialty food shop Dean & DeLuca in New York City, had heard about it from a customer in 1978. He ordered 120 cases from Modena, Italy, on a hunch and got it featured on the front page of the *New York Times* food section. Soon enough, every aspiring gourmet cook from New York to Los Angeles was in love with the stuff, and it became a kitchen staple.

If the Dean & DeLuca story was part of Zak and Stephen's hopes, it was also part of their strategy. "Early settlers and explorers were always writing back to the old country about foods they were discovering, like avocados, tomatoes, and mangos," explains Zak. "Today, there are still all of these things Americans have never tried, and we were convinced that one taste would make them fall in love." The duo had seen it firsthand: visitors to Punta Mona would enthusiastically sample the local fruit and often cite it as a highlight of their trip. The goal of the prototype phase was to figure out which of these exotic goods Americans would embrace as enthusiastically as they had balsamic vinegar. Would it be the banana vinegar? The guava preserves? The chocolate made with 100 percent cocoa?

Sourcing and packaging their first products also meant that they needed cash—and fast. They'd been relying on their savings, but Zak had reached the end of his money, and the rest of Stephen's financing was tied up in Punta Mona. Then, in an act of supreme luck, the company Zak held shares in from his software days was sold. Suddenly, his personal assets were liquid, and overnight his bank account balance went from zero to about $200,000. But the team still didn't have a business structure.

"I was just sort of throwing credit cards out paying for things, and Stephen was doing the same," explains Zak. "We were so invested in this idea, and of really changing people's lives, that we just dove in. It wasn't like, 'I gave $50,000 and you gave $50,000.' It was 'We're best friends and we're doing this thing.'" They even made it a family affair: Zak brought in his brother, Zev, who had a background in investing and business, while Stephen brought in his energetic father, Norman, a retired dentist. With four sets of hands on deck, they were ready to build their company. While the four would shift responsibility and scale their involvement up and down over the coming years—and eventually Stephen would step out of day-to-day operations to run Punta Mona full time again—they'd always stay true to their original goal of being equal cofounders and co-owners.

The Name Game

Two weeks before Zak was about to print the first batch of 10,000 labels, destined for items like coconut oil, cocoa powder, and the banana vinegar, he received an official-looking missive. It was a challenge to their trademark request from a restaurant with a similar name to their original moniker. "Everything else was set, we were this close to starting the presses, and we suddenly had no name," Zak recalls. "I was terrified."

Before a business can file for a trademark, it must first publish the name or phrase it wants to use. "It's one of those chicken–egg dilemmas you have to deal with early on," Zak explains. Do you file for the trademark as soon as possible, or do you start using the name and then establish ownership that way? And of course, a name is more than just a name: What does the brand mean, what does it look like, what's the tagline? After the summons, Zak spent ten days doing nothing but thinking about, talking about, asking about, and researching names. He was looking for something easy to pronounce yet exotic-sounding, food-friendly, and with no well-known meaning in the English language, so they could ascribe their own to it.

In the midst of all this, Stephen dragged Zak out to a local party so he would ostensibly take a night off. "But I was obsessed with the name, and continued to rack my brain, ignoring everyone there," he says. "I was being antisocial, to say the least." So when Stephen walked over and asked what Zak thought of Kopali, a woman at the party, Zak didn't catch the drift: Would he be interested in her, romantically? All Zak heard was the name. Kopali. It was what he'd been searching for.

Zak raced home to a computer and entered the name into a domain registry—it was available, and it didn't look like another brand had any sort of dibs on it. He realized Kopali was perfect in many ways: It starts with a K, which tends to be a strong winner for brands (Kellogg's, Kodak, and Kleenex, for example). Kopali is relatively short but has three syllables, a tenet of memorable names (like Amazon, McDonald's, and Microsoft). And as Zak excitedly traced the word's roots to its indigenous Mexican origins, he found that it referred to the resin, or lifeblood, of a big rain forest tree.

All Zak had to do was look over to the painting they'd already commissioned to adorn their packaging: a big rain forest tree, spreading out over the jungle. Hello, Kopali.

Launch Big or Go Home

In the end, it was almost two years after Whole Foods had said "go for it!" that the first Kopali products were ready: They had the name, the goods, the labels, the shipping processes. What else did they need? Then the marketing director of Whole Foods called and asked how they planned to support the launch. "We didn't even know what she meant!" Zak says with a laugh. They quickly learned that it was the brand's responsibility to create promotions and signage and support the sale of its products with demos and coupons. For example, Whole Foods was going to give them end caps, the high exposure space at the end of aisles that are filled with new, seasonal, or big sale items. Think of the placement of Halloween candy or door-buster deals; you can't miss them and are impulsively tempted to buy. For a few weeks, Kopali's line of fruit, chocolate, and more would have that premium, coveted spot—but those few weeks would also be their sole chance to make a splash.

"It turns out that marketing—getting people to notice and buy your product once it hits shelves—is more important than how delicious your product is," explains Zak. "It's more important than how moving your story is. It's more important than your great name or your colorful, meaning-packed packaging." The truth about food retailing comes down to this: Good retailers have products overflowing out of every corner of every shelf in every store. They won't put something on those shelves that can't be sold, and if they do, it's instantly replaced with a product that does sell. And it's onto those overloaded shelves that thousands and thousands of new products are introduced every week.

Some of those products come from small entrepreneurs with an inspiring brand and a lot of energy. And some of those products come from giant food companies that are constantly forced to innovate; grow their lines; increase their shelf space; and compete with the other cereals, chips, and preserves. The goal, explains Zak, is to get your product *on* the shelf, get your product *off* that shelf, and then get your product reordered and *back* on that shelf.

But the Kopali team knew none of this when it was asked that pivotal question, "What are you going to do to support the line?" In response, Zak and Stephen decided to have a little fun. Earlier, they had driven all the way from California to Costa Rica on a bus that ran on repurposed vegetable oil and were amazed at the attention it brought. "People and the media loved it—it's the bus that runs on garbage!" says Zak. Could Kopali go big and kick off the launch with a similar bus tour?

They spent about $50,000 and renovated a used bus with donations and help from friends and other earth-conscious companies, using eco-friendly materials like bamboo, coconut wood, and recycled plastic. They reconfigured the engine to run on used vegetable oil, which they'd pick up, gratis, from restaurants. Then they loaded the bus with samples and supplies—they'd sleep on the bus wherever they could park on the cheap—and drove from Whole Foods to Whole Foods all over Los Angeles, San Diego, Phoenix, and Las Vegas.

Each location was now featuring a Kopali end cap, stocked with more than twenty different products. The Kopali team would set up bright and early with a sampling tent in the parking lot and a demo table inside. From opening until closing, Zak, Stephen, and their friends would tell the Kopali story, show pictures of the farmers, and give customers free tastes of their treats. Zak would also call the local media and invite them to come on over. In most places, reporters would show up, and Kopali and its crazy bus would be on TV that night. The next day, Zak and Stephen would drive to another Whole Foods and do it all over again. "We banked completely on this effort and made it bigger than could possibly be justified," says Zak. "But, miraculously, it sort of worked. It put us on the map and our products started moving off the shelves."

Kopali, Take Two

That is, *some* of their products were moving. It didn't take long for Zak and Stephen to look at their banana vinegar plan with a critical eye and realize they'd made a mistake. When they were dreaming up their business in Costa Rica, they hadn't considered how hard it is to get someone to try a completely unfamiliar product, especially a new vinegar. "It's not even a marketing challenge—it's more of a 'mission: almost impossible,'" explains a now-wiser Zak. "But let's say you do get someone to purchase a bottle. It was expensive and they had never heard of it, but somehow you convinced them to buy. Maybe you were giving sample tastes, maybe the retailer helped you with a promotion, maybe their mom tried it on a trip to Costa Rica. And let's say the customer took it home and loved it."

Here's the problem: that customer is never going to buy the vinegar again. A month will pass, two months, and even if it's just a small amount, that bottle of vinegar sitting in the pantry is not what's called a rapid-turnover product. Rapid turnover became Kopali's first big business lesson. The term refers to a product that customers buy again and again—say, milk, cereal, salsa, and cheese. It's used up quickly, and if customers like it, they're putting it in their shopping cart every week. At the opposite end of the spectrum is vinegar. Like most pantry items, it has slow turnover (think ketchup, mustard, and honey and

WHY A SOCIAL MISSION IS GOOD FOR BUSINESS

Thirty years ago, Paul Newman was thinking about bottling up and selling his famous salad dressing. Then the legendary film star had a bigger idea: he'd give it all away. By *it*, he meant the profits from the sale of the dressings, and today he's known as the founding father of the concept that a company can exist solely for social good. To date, sales of Newman's Own dressings, tomato sauce, and Fig Newmans have resulted in a $350 million donation—every single penny of after-tax profits—distributed to hundreds of charities.

Should you add social responsibility to your company's values? If you listen to multiple large-scale studies on corporate citizenship, the answer is a resounding yes. According to a Cone Corporate Citizenship Study, "Building Brand Trust," 43 percent of Americans purchase products from a company after hearing about its commitment to social issues, 43 percent tell friends or family, and *28 percent intentionally pay more for a product that supports a social issue.* The same study identifies education, health, and the environment as the three core issues customers are most likely to support.

Ready to get started? Consider these questions:

1. What will your focus be? Will you partner with an existing nonprofit, or support various charities? Will you work social good into your company's purchasing criteria, buying fair trade or other sustainably sourced items? Will you encourage your employees to volunteer or take on pro bono projects?

2. Will you donate money? Will it be product (such as matching every product sold with an equal donation to a community in need, like TOMS shoes and Warby Parker glasses do)? Will it be proceeds (the full purchase price of an item), or profits (the percentage that remains after business costs like salaries and taxes) from a particular item? Will it be a dollar amount of each product sold? Will it be a percentage of sales or profits from your business as a whole (like the 1% for the Planet coalition)? Will it be an annual lump-sum donation? No matter what you decide to donate, focus on transparency, both in your relationship with partner nonprofits and with your customers.

3. Will you donate time and expertise? Can you partner on an event with your chosen charity? Give them products to use? Work with them in other ways, such as mentoring a student through an education charity? Set up community centers or other resources in the places you source your raw ingredients from?

4. How will you let customers know about your social outreach? Will you communicate through on-product branding and education? Website and social media campaigns? If you give away money or support social good and no one knows, it's not beneficial to your company. Think about how you can tell the world about your good outreach.

bags of rice, flour, and sugar). For a fledgling food entrepreneur, slow turnover items are *exactly* the products to avoid.

"Even with all of my Internet research, I had never thought of it," says Zak. Today, it would be one of the first questions he'd consider, How easy it is to get people to try a product; and if they try it and love it, how likely are they to buy it again very quickly? Those criteria would influence all of Kopali's future products. While Zak and Stephen were tirelessly supporting their products, tweaking the current line, and attempting to hang on to the small inroads they'd made, they were also considering how should they move forward.

They leveraged their initial success to maneuver their way into an informational meeting with the global purchasing coordinator for Whole Foods, an especially unusual and impressive feat because most Whole Foods buying is done on a regional level. They went through their usual pitch, but the purchasing coordinator wasn't sold. "I love what you're doing, but I'm not interested in any of your products," he said. The letdown was fast and hard hitting, until he continued on with what would foretell Kopali's direction: "What I'd love is this emotional pull, but with snacks. If you could do that with a more tightly edited line, I'd launch it nationally."

"That was the direction he gave us," says Zak. "Single-serve, rapid turnover, very emotionally charged items. But it still needed to include the same ingredients, the same story, and the same essence of Kopali. That was our challenge." This time around, everything was much more intentional and strategic. "We had some experience, more great thinkers on our team, a little bit of real investment money, and of course, substantial feedback from Whole Foods," says Zak. Within a year, they relaunched with a line of ten easily identifiable Kopali products: two-ounce, $3.99 bags of exotic dried fruits like mulberries and chocolate treats made with espresso beans, dried banana, and cocoa nibs. In 2008, Whole Foods put them at every one of its checkout counters in the United States.

Kopali, Take Three

After the auspicious relaunch, Stephen headed back to Punta Mona and his educational center, while Zak and new president Jacqueline Holmes took on the day-to-day responsibilities of Kopali. In 2011, they began to suspect that selling both chocolate confections and dried fruits was confusing Kopali's messaging. Customers saw dried fruit as a healthy pantry item—something that was much cheaper in the bulk bins than in Kopali's little packs. "If the fruit wasn't 'worth it,' what would they think about the chocolate?" says Zak. The fruit was being viewed as a commodity item, something sold only on the basis of price, like a bushel of corn. Zak didn't want that perception to affect sales of the chocolate.

Plus, the fruits didn't fit Kopali's strategy of selling impulse treats because they were being sold in the interior aisles, instead of at the checkout line. In the aisles, customers are looking at their shopping lists and picking up the items they'll use to feed their families. In the midst of $1-per-pound chicken and huge boxes of cereal, a little bag of fruit selling for $3.99 doesn't look like a value. But when shoppers are checking out, they've accomplished their task and have collected the food they need to make healthy, affordable meals. "It's treat yourself time," says Zak. "And among the generic candies, our little bag of special chocolate pops right out."

By 2012, Kopali knew that their big play would be chocolate. They'd focus their limited resources on their truly superstar products and begin to phase out their less-successful fruit line. Today, it's all about chocolate: dark chocolate, banana chocolate, coffee chocolate, and chocolate chocolate. "We're selling one thing: your healthy, sustainable, exotic, fancy chocolate," says Zak. "That's brand-able; you can wrap your head around it. You'll buy it for a night at the opera, a snack after yoga, or a treat for a car trip. It's an impulse purchase that makes you feel good about yourself because it's delicious, pure, and supports people around the world."

Seven years after Zak and Stephen had first talked into the night about the horrific pesticides being dropped all over Costa Rica, Kopali was solving the problem that had started their adventure. While their initial banana vinegar idea wasn't a winner, their organic, fair trade, storytelling idea was; they just had to find the right product to pair it with. Now Kopali is supporting indigenous farmers around the world by sourcing sustainable chocolate and fillings and selling the candy as a premium, specialty, feel-good treat. There's just one thing left to do: create markets for more organic farmers, in more places, and continue to use the power of business to change the world.

TAKE AWAY

- **Think rapid-turnover, nonperishable, value-added products.** You want rapid turnover so customers buy the product again and again, not just yearly. Nonperishable items are easier to ship and distribute, and value-added products (as opposed to commodity products) let you command a premium price in the market.
- **Be willing to shift direction.** The Whole Foods buyer loved Kopali's storytelling mission and brand but wanted to pair that with snacks instead of pantry items, like vinegar and jams. By tweaking its products, Kopali was able to move into a new category and succeed. What adjacent categories might your brand work well in?
- **Eventually, focus on your superstar items.** Single-serve, Fair Trade, organic chocolate was a winning solution for Kopali, so the company ultimately stopped selling the other items and focused on one successful line.

3

Creating and Evolving a Brand

TASTY

Best friends Shannan Swanson and Liane Weintraub turn their evangelical passion for organic kids' food into a fun gummy snacks business.

Friends First

Enter the buzzing universe of a food trade show, and it won't take you long to find Tasty cofounders Shannan Swanson and Liane Weintraub. Dressed in white jeans and bright blue matching Tasty T-shirts, they're the fun, popular kids you want to hang out with, and everyone in the convention center seems to know them. Beyond the outfits, their close bond is evident as they trip over one another's words and enthusiastically nod along as the other speaks.

Long before they started a business, however, before the children who inspired their food even came along, these entrepreneurs were simply great friends navigating their twenties in Los Angeles. Both were passionate about food: Shannan had trained as a chef at Le

Stuart Gow

Liane Weintraub (left) and Shannan Swanson

Cordon Bleu and Liane was a broadcast journalist who tracked down hard-hitting agricultural stories. Both spent hours cooking for their "wild and outrageous" dinner parties, and creating delicious, healthy, and sustainable meals for their friends became a way of life.

But when they had their first babies, Shannan and Liane were dismayed at the baby food they found at their local supermarkets. It was often filled with sugar and preservatives, and buying organic was not even an option; it didn't exist. So they began to make their own, dreaming up and pureeing combinations of fruits and vegetables that they deemed worthy of their little ones' developing taste buds.

And they began to talk, simply hypothetically, about selling this healthier baby food. Shannan was running a small catering business and thought her clients would love something like it; Liane backed her friend up and helped her brainstorm. "I wasn't thinking I'd be a part of it, I just wanted to encourage Shannan to try," she remembers. Then Shannan read about a line of new, natural baby foods in a magazine and was spurred from talk into action. She immediately called Liane. "If we don't do this now, we're going to regret it forever. Our chance is slipping away!"

After thinking it over for just a few hours, Liane intentionally called Shannan when she wouldn't be able to answer the phone; she was going to propose something big and didn't want her friend to feel obligated to say yes. She left a voicemail: "All right, I thought about it and if this is really a business you want to try, then I will do it with you. We don't have to, and if you're not interested forget I ever mentioned it." Shannan called back within minutes. "Let's do it!" she exclaimed. Tasty Brand had begun.

We Have a Great Idea—Now What?!

Their let's-do-it attitude became the defining mantra of their new business. "And that doesn't always make things easy," Liane says, laughing. "We had no idea how to start. Making baby food isn't rocket science: You cook two or three types of organic produce, then puree and freeze the blends. But as soon as we left our own kitchens, we were in foreign territory. How on earth do you do scale up?" Their list of questions was long: How and where could they buy the ingredients in bulk? How would they find a facility? What kind of kitchen appliances did they need?

The irony was that everyone expected them to be well connected and know all of the answers. Shannan's grandfather had founded

Swanson & Sons and invented the frozen chicken pot pie as well as the first commercial chicken broth. But the business had been sold decades earlier, and Shannan's father, who did know the ins and outs of the food business, had died fifteen years before. "We realized we knew absolutely no one in the food industry," Shannan says. "We were going to have to do it just like anyone else did."

Their first breakthrough was finding a natural food products trade show, Natural Products Expo East. Expo East and Expo West are the two major trade shows for the natural foods industry (go to expoeast.com and expowest.com for details on attending) and are held every fall in Baltimore, Maryland, and every spring in Anaheim, California. They're an opportunity to showcase raw ingredients and final products, so many food businesses meet with both ends of their chain—ingredient suppliers and supermarket buyers—at the same show. (The other dominant trade shows are sponsored by the National Association of Fancy Food [NASFT] and are colloquially referred to as the Fancy Food Shows. They're held in San Francisco in the winter and New York City in the summer. Go to nasft.org for more information.)

They found out about Expo East just a few weeks before that year's Baltimore show, and immediately decided to fly out. It wasn't an easy trip; Shannan was pregnant; Liane was nursing; and the friends wandered around the packed floor, completely clueless. But they hadn't come all that way to waste an opportunity. They shook off their inhibitions and walked right up to vendors to ask for advice. "I have a real soft spot for people who do that today," Liane says, "because the people who helped us there were few and far between."

But the questions began to pay off. Liane approached one vendor who sold bulk produce and asked, "You have organic this and organic that. How would we be able to buy some?" The friends realized that they were nobody to him, not the type of major customer he really needed to woo. He said he couldn't discuss the possibilities on the busy show floor, but then he added, "Maybe you'll come and visit the farm in Oregon sometime." That was all Shannan and Liane needed. Two days later, they called and said they would be coming up in a week. Was that OK?

The friends road-tripped hundreds of miles from Los Angeles up to the farm and so shocked the vendor that he actually sold them products and became their first official supplier. That initial contact was enormously helpful ("There are no Yellow Pages for this!" says Liane) and led them on a trail toward other answers about packaging, co-packers, and more. Today, they look back at that first trade show experience as the starting point, when their dream started to shift into reality.

As their product came together, the one thing they needn't have worried about was keeping it a secret. "We wouldn't reveal to anyone—even to our manufacturers or suppliers—what we were making. We were hysterically secretive and convinced that we were going to be a massive overnight success," says Shannan. In reality, their initial idea was just a first step in the evolution of their business. (Spoiler alert: It's not even the product they sell today!) "Now we're like, 'Go do it! Steal our idea!'" says Liane. "You still have to design the branding, make the product, come up with a marketing scheme, get the grocery store placement. The idea is the seed, but it's what you do with that idea that's important."

Taking Care of Business

As they tackled the logistics of their physical product, the pair was also setting up a legal partnership. Liane's husband, a real estate

LEGAL COMMANDMENTS FOR START-UPS

Nathan Whitehouse, an attorney who works with early-stage companies at Whitehouse Law, PLLC, in New York City shares the first things he'd tell all new entrepreneurs to consider.

1. Talk to a lawyer as soon as you can—and long before you start making your first products. There's a lot of risk and uncertainty involved with a new business, and not a lot of cash for things like a lawyer! But the more you're hyperdisciplined and get legal issues settled at the very beginning, the more you're going to increase your likelihood of success.

2. Find a lawyer you trust. You're relying on this person to provide business counsel, so you need to trust his or her judgment and know he or she is looking out for your best interest. Start with word-of-mouth recommendations from other consumer product entrepreneurs, then consider three things: First, a good match is partially about personality. Second, find a lawyer who handles start-ups, because it's a specialized skill set. Finally, your lawyer should be connected to the type of people you want to meet and be willing to make introductions.

3. Make sure you own your logo. I can't count the number of times I've had a food entrepreneur come to me—somebody with a really fantastic idea and product—who had a friend put together a logo. Now the business is taking off, and it's unclear how things are divided among all parties. Have your friend sign an agreement up front and specifically transfer the copyrights of the design to you (you can even Google agreement templates). Otherwise, the product name, design, and logo belong to him or her by default, and you might have to trade a big chunk of equity to retain rights.

4. Forget a patent—make sure you have trade secrets. It's really important to keep those trade secrets (such as your recipes or how you produce your product) confidential, or you won't receive the protection the law provides. Anyone who ever works with your recipe needs to sign a nondisclosure agreement and understand that it belongs exclusively to the company. Established trade secrets, like KFC's Original Recipe spice blend, can be worth millions of dollars but you get legal protection only if you've kept your secret the entire time.

5. Not every name can be trademarked. There are a lot of archaic rules surrounding what's trademark-able and what's not. The name can't be a word people associate with the type of product itself; you can't trademark a banana brand named Bananas, for example. You also need a name that's unique from existing names, including anything similar. Start by searching at the U.S. Patent and Trademark Office website, and then a lawyer can run more exhaustive searches through specialized databases.

6. Register your business, even if you're a mom-and-pop joint. Your financing plans will usually determine which category you choose: limited liability companies (LLCs) are better for smaller businesses without large capital needs, and corporations are better if you need to raise a significant amount of money. If you want to grow aggressively, a corporation will give you the structural support to manage the relationships between the founder, cofounder, early-stage employees, and investors.

7. Sit down with all possible business partners, whether they're friends, a colleague, or a spouse, at the very beginning. Decide how much time, personal money, connections, and passion each person is going to put into the business. Force yourselves to come up with a breakdown. It's really common for people to come to me after they've been working on a project for a while. Everyone's been getting along, and then the crucial conversation comes up. One person says, "I think I should get 99.99 percent because I've been spending so much time on this," and the business partner says, "Are you crazy?" A lawyer can tell you what equity shares make sense in your situation for different stakeholders: everyone from founders to advisory board members to someone who makes a couple of phone calls for you.

developer, referred them to a business attorney who drafted a limited liability company agreement. Their plan was to split everything fifty-fifty, but the lawyer told them they'd have to do more than just verbally state their intent; they needed a full partnership contract.

"Of course, we just wanted to rely on our history as best friends; we wouldn't do anything to hurt each other!" recalls Liane. But they understood the practicalities of having such a document and worked out pages of nitty-gritty details about the potential, possible, eventual dissolution of either their business or their partnership—essentially, a prenuptial agreement for the business world. "It was like negotiating your divorce when you're madly in love!" remembers Shannan. "It's obviously not an everyday occurrence for good friends to enter into a commitment involving legal documents, conflict resolution clauses, and tie-breaker voting protocol. It really forced us to look at our friendship and evaluate it, which I believe has made us stronger friends."

And over the years, they've learned that a business partnership is even more like a marriage contract than they originally thought: they both have a lot invested in their venture, know everything about the other, and feel the depth of their mutual goals. "What Liane and I have is the only thing that's comparable to the relationship I have with my husband," says Shannan. "But we're still actual friends, in the same way you're still friends with your husband even when you become partners in parenthood, house care, etc." And they don't turn and run in opposite directions as soon as the workday is done; the friends are just as likely to round up their kids and husbands and head out for a group dinner.

Calling in the Branding Big Guns

Soon Shannan and Liane had legal contracts, a start-up loan from a bank, and a way to manufacture their baby food. Then came the most important part: branding. They met with brand strategist Susan White, who helps incubate brands in the early stages, and excitedly began telling her about their ideas for flavors and retail packaging.

Susan brought the discussion to a screeching halt—they had the process all backward. "Forget that. *First*, you have to decide who you are and what's important to you as a brand," she said. "What's your identity? What makes you who you are?" This wasn't going to be a thirty-minute session—in, out, done—but a months-long process. They essentially underwent what Liane calls "psychoanalysis for your brand identity," to develop three brand attributes: genuine, all-organic, and fun. Once they had crystallized what they stood for, nothing was arbitrary: Everything from their visual look and name to endorsements and verbal message had to tie back to those traits.

The pair ran through a multitude of exercises, trying their brand on for authenticity and consumer appeal. They looked at hundreds of other brands, figuring out what parts of the messages they liked, and what they'd do differently. For example, picking their trademark color, vibrant turquoise, was both personal and practical. Although it had been a favorite hue of both for years, their choice was also deliberate; most of the organic product packaging at the time was brown, green, or black. "It was like an unwritten rule that organic products had to be packaged in kraft paper and tied with twine!" says Liane. Their response was to run in the other direction, picking an exciting and colorful shade that didn't scream earthy.

The final brand philosophy they came up with was a combination of a 100 percent organic and sustainable product with a fun, childlike feeling, the type that makes you want to watch cartoons in your pajamas and eat sugary cereal. "At the time, organic was everything but fun. It was serious. It was responsible," Liane explains. They wanted to have that same do-good vibe underneath—say, by using eco-friendly recycled paper with vegetable-based inks—but with festive colors and living-out-loud vibe. And the name of all this sustainable fun? Tasty, of course.

Pivoting the Brand: Tasty 2.0

Nine months after that first, "Let's do it!" Liane and Shannan were ready to launch. After an early rush of publicity (including mentions in *W* and *InStyle*), they had brand recognition but were stocked in just a few regional stores. Although their baby food purees were well received, they couldn't get the space in store freezers they'd hoped for, and distributing a frozen product was proving difficult. So over the next year, they took their rock-solid brand identity ("We realized that this was why we had spent so much time on it!" says Shannan) and transitioned into their second product: organic fruit snacks.

Tasty Brand 2.0 started simply: The friends were giving their kids a gummy vitamin each morning to make sure they were getting all of the nutrients they needed. But the kids didn't see them as medicinal but as candy! A gummy a day soon led to begging sessions for more, but too many meant an overload of vitamins. Shannan and Liane were commiserating about their struggles when the obvious answer struck: What if they made fruit snacks that also contained 100 percent of the recommended daily vitamin allowance for children? They did a little research and found there was a hole in the market just waiting to be filled with organic, natural gummy snacks: All of the options in conventional supermarkets were packed with high fructose corn syrup or artificial colors and flavors. They realized that a dose of vitamins would just be a bonus: Tasty's real selling point was about simply getting rid of the junk in a favorite snack.

Although the Tasty branding was in place, Liane and Shannan would have to start their new manufacturing process from scratch. This time, they worked with a co-packer, a business that manufactures food on behalf of various food and drink companies. How did they know if a sample passed muster? When their kids liked a flavor as much as the other treats they clamored for, like cheesy chips. But forget about the kids—the Tasty founders say they themselves love the gummies a little *too* much. "We have to keep our research and development samples under lock and key at the office, because we snack on them so much!" Shannan says, laughing.

Formulating flavors for those research samples is where Shannan's chef training comes in handy. Her years in the kitchen taught her to mix only fruits with a natural affinity, whether by geographic area or season (mango-apple-peach would be a no-go). Instead, their line includes straight-up flavors like peach, tangerine, and lemon, all in true-to-life shapes. The pair stays away from anything that tastes artificial, even if it's not. "We were surprised that some natural flavors

THE SEVEN-STEP PLAN TO DIY PUBLIC RELATIONS

Publicist Thea Zagata knows firsthand that the large monthly retainers most PR firms require are unrealistic for a start-up: While running her cookie business, she did all of her outreach herself. Now her DIY PR kits for small entrepreneurs let you smartly tackle PR on your own (go to Pescepr.com for a customized kit). She shares her plan:

1. Define exactly who your target audience is. For example, I marketed my cookies as party favors and presents, so I wanted to reach:

- Brides
- Affluent women aged twenty-three to fifty-five, including women planning lots of big parties: birthdays, showers, bachelorettes
- Young men aged twenty to forty who would be buying Valentine's Day gifts

2. Find your media targets based on your target audience. In addition to searching online, stop by a bookstore and review their magazine and newspaper selection. What is your target audience reading? For my cookie business target audiences, I wanted to get coverage in these types of publications:

- Brides—*Brides, Martha Stewart Weddings, The Knot*
- Affluent women aged twenty-three to fifty-five—*Real Simple; O, the Oprah Magazine; Daily Candy*
- Young men—*Maxim, Esquire*

3. Build a media list. Research the email addresses and phone numbers for the appropriate editor or writer at the publications and blogs you're targeting. Go to mastheadsonline.blogspot.com to look up magazine contacts, then ed2010.com to find the email address templates for each company. Record this information on an Excel spreadsheet so you can easily keep track of your interaction with each contact (for example, emailed on 9/14; met with product samples on 10/11). You should also regularly read the blogs and magazines on your media wish list so you can be familiar with their content. Never spam a list of hundreds of writers with the hope that a few journalists will be interested. Remember: quality, not quantity.

4. Determine your media hook or angle. Is it a new product? After the initial launch, do you have a new line? Does the product tie into a holiday? With my cookie company, I frequently pitched seasonal stories, such as holiday gift guides and summer entertaining. Think: Why should writers care? What's new/different/unique about your product? Does it fit into a new trend?

5. Write a press release. People often find this intimidating, but think of it as a one-page story about your product and company. What's the founder's story? Where can you buy the product? What makes it unique? How much does it cost? Include all the information that a journalist might need. A press release can also serve double-duty for search engine optimization for your website: Include your website's keywords and submit the press release to a wire service, such as PRWeb.com. It costs about $200 (look for a coupon code for a discount), but it's nice layer to a targeted campaign and can help your website gain a higher ranking for online searches.

6. Invest in four or five good photographs of your product. I recommend looking for a professional photographer on Craigslist or posting an ad at a nearby art or design school. You can hire a student who wants to build a portfolio for a nominal fee.

7. Finally, it's time for media outreach (or pitching). I like to write a very brief email note and then follow up with the press release and samples if there's interest. In the pitch note, you want to explain who you are and why the writer should pay attention. Include a single low-resolution picture if it helps explain the product. A week later, follow up on your first email (resend the same email with an additional sentence). A single phone call a week after that is fine, and then, if there's no interest, drop that angle. In a few months you can try again with a different angle. And if there *is* interest, congratulations! You now have a media contact and can start working together to feature your product in his or her publication.

taste artificial and vice versa!" says Shannan. "Strawberry, for example, is very hard to do naturally. So we stick with flavors that we can actually replicate in candy form."

The gummies went over well with not only kids but also with adults, who began purchasing them and becoming the not-so-secret consumers. Shannan and Liane even created a tagline to appeal to this customer demographic: "Organic snacks for kids 2 to 102." For example, their Splash gummies, enhanced with electrolytes, found a surprising following in the skateboard and triathlete communities. Today, they no longer make any baby food and instead focus solely on organic gummies and cookies.

The Power of Passion

After their second-time's-the-charm launch, Tasty started to grow in both size and popularity. The secret to their success is loud and clear: having a strong brand; advocating a product they believe in; and focusing on energetic, enthusiastic public relations. Their public relations strategy is informal: the goal is to connect with people who have influence in their own sphere, whether that's traditional print media, buyers from grocery stores, or local mommy bloggers—anyone who can spread the word to loyal followers. "You can't, as hard as you try, go out and meet every single one of your would-be customers," Shannan says. "But you *can* meet the influencers they're listening to." The friends love social media; it allows them to connect with more and more of their customers directly and personally. Liane, who does the overwhelming majority of Tasty's Twitter and Facebook outreach herself, credits their engaged following to the fact that it's actually the Tasty founders behind the screen. It leads to a genuine community. Giveaways are part of their approach, but so is straight-up, no-gifts-attached chatting.

Today, the Tasty founders would tell budding entrepreneurs to pace themselves with traditional media outreach (magazines, morning TV shows, and so on) but to go big in social media. It's a lesson they learned the hard way during their baby food days: Mainstream media coverage sounds great, but you need to have national distribution to match. Otherwise, people hear about your product but can't easily buy it, and the opportunity is lost. But with social media, you get chances over and over and over again.

Finally, they credit their success to straight-up "holding our feet to the fire. That's what helps us get things done," Shannan says. "We announce it and own it, and it's a way of holding ourselves accountable." For example, in 2011, the pair first learned about GMOs at a food convention they were attending. GMO refers to genetically modified organisms, plants whose DNA has been shifted and changed to resist pesticides and insecticides. Three of the most common GMO crops—corn, sugar beets, and soybeans—end up in most of the American food supply.

The health and environmental effects of GMOs are not yet known, but in their current form they go against the ideals of the organic food movement. "We immediately, and very publicly, committed to being GMO-free," Liane says. She calls the overhaul and certification process "gut wrenching"—every single ingredient had to be meticulously tracked and traced—but within six months all Tasty products were verified by the Non-GMO Project. "Did we get extra gray hairs? Yes," she says. "Was it worth it? Of course."

Unlike Liane and Shannan, seasoned businesspeople probably wouldn't have publicly announced they were throwing their hat in the non-GMO ring. Instead, it would have been an internal decision and approached quietly, lessening the risk of an embarrassing backtrack. But the Tasty founders were true to their let's-do-it roots and shouted from the mountaintops. "That's why we started this business—to change the types of food we could give to our kids," says Liane. "And we can only do that if we take risks and act on what we believe." It's a strategy they plan to continue as their kids, and their business, grow up.

TAKE AWAY

- **Focus on designing your brand just as much as your product.** Even if the product doesn't work out—maybe there's not a market for it or it's difficult to scale or distribute—any work you put into a strong brand can be transferred to a whole array of similar products in the future.
- **Decide who you are and what's important to you as a brand.** What's your identity? What three words would sum up your brand philosophy? (Tasty picked genuine, organic, and fun.)
- **Always come back to the branding.** Everything from packaging and public relations outreach to flavor development and hiring employees should be on-brand. Tasty kept their fun vibe alive at trade shows, on social media, and in their flavors and design.

4

Secrets of Food Safety and Scale

EVOL

Avid rock climber Phil Anson makes all-natural burritos—first for his climbing buddies and then for the world.

Burritos, Anyone?

Phil Anson had just one goal when he started selling burritos out of the back of his car: to make enough money to support his passion for rock climbing. He could cook the burritos in the morning, sell them at lunch, and spend the whole afternoon climbing in the Colorado mountains—what a lifestyle! The new college grad had recently quit his job as a line cook at an upscale Denver restaurant and was ready for better hours and more sunlight.

Inspiration struck on a trip to Joshua Tree National Park with friends: "We spent our days and nights outside, rock climbing and camping, and I realized that I just wanted to climb—and climbing made me think of an idea to support myself, because what were we

Courtesy Evol

Phil Anson

eating? Lots and lots of burritos," says Phil. He tossed the idea out to his buddies. "What if I made burritos and sold them to climbers? If I can sell 500 burritos in a week, I can pay my rent and buy groceries. This should be easy!"

Phil's logic went straight to the heart of his own experience. He and his housemates were always putting on burrito nights for their friends, whether they were at home in Boulder or out camping. "The whole idea is so low-key and friendly," says Phil. "Lay out a bunch of different fillings and let everyone wrap his or her own combination up in a tortilla." Their love of burritos coincided with a trend that was about to go national; the first Chipotle Mexican Grill restaurants opened near campus when Phil was attending Denver University in the late 1990s, and by the early 2000s the chain would start expanding across the United States. "Today, Chipotles are everywhere, but back then, no one knew—or at least, I didn't know!—that this burrito thing was going to get so big," he says. "I wasn't a sophisticated entrepreneur, saying, 'Ah, there's a gap in the market for burritos.' It was like, 'I like burritos. Everyone likes burritos. I bet I can make $500 a week so I can rock climb a lot.'"

Phil wasn't armed with a business plan or financial savvy, just good old kitchen skills from his years as a line cook. He drove to Costco and bought ingredients, then went to work in his cabin, boiling beans and making green chile sauce. He'd wrap the finished hot burritos in foil, put them in a cooler so they'd stay warm, and head out to the Eldorado Springs climbing area parking lot. Phil approached cars as people unloaded their gear: "Hey, anybody want to buy a burrito? Just two bucks!" In return, he got confused, wary looks; no one was quite sure what he was doing or who this guy was. Suffice it to say, after two days and a mere few dollars' worth of sales, he wasn't exactly selling out.

Hmmm. If selling hot burritos out of a cooler wasn't a thing in Eldorado Springs, what else could Phil do? Going door to door (or in this case, store to store) felt intimidating. But were there other casual places where people didn't have access to hot food? Construction sites! So Phil staked out some spots, rolled up, pulled out his cooler, and tried again, this time speaking in Spanish. But just like the rock climbers, the construction workers were confused. Who was this guy? And why was he waving foil packets around? Phil mentally crossed "construction sites" off his list.

Next, he tried the Denver bar scene—drunk people like burritos, right? "That actually kind of worked," says Phil. "When people came out of the bars at 2 a.m., starving, they'd go for my big, cheesy, $2 burritos." But after a few evenings, he realized that the late nights weren't any better than his restaurant days. Plus, "sells burritos to drunk people in the middle of the night" didn't sound like the type of career plan he was after.

Phil was back to square one. On his way home, he stopped by the Eldorado Corner Market to grab a cup of coffee. "What am I going to do?" he thought. "I've already put $300 into this thing, and now I have no job *and* no money." As he walked out of the store he passed the refrigerator case, which proudly featured a few premade sandwiches. The shocker was that they looked semi-homemade; they had labels, but were covered in regular plastic wrap. "They weren't sophisticated," says Phil. "I'd call them semi-legit, a step up from what I was doing. And all of a sudden I realized that *I* could do that."

Phil raced back to his cabin and whipped up packaging. It took him all of ten seconds to decide on a name for his burritos: Phil's Fresh Foods. He wrapped his hand-drawn labels around the burritos and headed out. He had no idea what his costs were. He had no idea what price to charge. He didn't know what the laws were. He just drove back to the market, asked to talk to the owner, gave him the samples, and sold his first few burritos. The corner station would pay Phil $1.65 per burrito, and sell them for $3.00. "I was so surprised—it was easy!" says Phil.

When Phil called the manager at the Corner Market, he found that his burritos had sold, and the manager was happy to take a few more. And each day, the store would sell a handful of Phil's refrigerated burritos, and he kept making and delivering fresh batches. And thus was born Phil's company. He went out and started talking to other gas station–type places and coffee shops, and by the end of the first month he had about ten customers who were each buying $100 of burritos a week. Phil was actually generating some revenue!

An Adventure in Fresh Food Safety

After a few weeks of regular sales, Phil knew he couldn't continue making the burritos in his cabin's makeshift kitchen. Whatever the laws were, he had a suspicion he wasn't following them. Phil dropped by a local culinary school, the Cooking School of the Rockies, and asked the receptionist at the front desk if anybody knew where he could rent some kitchen space.

The chefs directed Phil to Out to Lunch Sandwich, where the owners agreed to rent him a prep table for $12 an hour. Phil moved in and gained more than just kitchen space: the owners also became his mentors, guiding him through the basic quandaries of a small food business. They introduced him to food suppliers, taught him how to write invoices, and helped him register with the city health department.

Within a few months, Phil's Fresh Foods was bringing in more and more accounts, and Phil was making a commensurate amount of burritos. "I was growing my business very aggressively," he says. "I was young and had unlimited energy, making burritos at all hours of the night and never sleeping." In fact, he had taken over the whole kitchen, and the $12 an hour rent he was charged no longer made sense. When the owners suggested a rate that was more market price, Phil readily agreed. And he happily stayed on, using the kitchen as his own facility, until the U.S. Department of Agriculture (USDA) came to visit.

Phil was cooking away one day when a USDA inspector showed up at the sandwich shop kitchen. "You can't operate like this," he told Phil. He explained that because Phil was selling meat products wholesale—to convenience stores and coffee shops and not just direct to consumers—he had to cook in an official USDA-inspected facility, not a regular commercial kitchen.

"Like so many of the bumps in the road you experience as a young business, this felt like the end of the world at the time," says Phil. "But in retrospect, I should've been flattered I was even on the USDA's radar; I was still only making a couple hundred burritos a week." Luckily, there was a certified USDA facility nearby, and the owner agreed to make room for Phil. He started making fresh, meat-filled burritos again, this time with a USDA stamp of approval on each package.

Phil had thought he knew a lot about food safety from his days in restaurant kitchens—principles like not cross-contaminating cooked meat with raw meat—but quickly realized that manufacturing rules are much more complex. "When you start out, you think, 'Oh, I'm just making a burrito. I know how to sauté meat,'" he says. But the industry standards and regulations are both time and capital intensive. Plus, there are specific risks associated with both meat and ready-to-eat, limited-shelf-life products.

It turned out that making a meat burrito is radically different and exponentially more complicated than making, say, cookies. Today, Phil and his team write and implement extremely detailed safety plans, some of which are 300 pages long! While these regulations exist to some extent in all food businesses, the level of scientific detail and oversight is much more complex for a fresh food product.

First, your product has to undergo considerable shelf-life testing, and then you devise ways to protect against any microorganisms that develop. Once you have reams of scientific data, you defend your product and methods to the USDA and FDA. This whole process isn't about quality control; it's purely about food safety. On the other hand, canned, frozen, or shelf-stable products might deteriorate in cosmetic or taste ways, but they won't have as many food safety issues. (The "Best

By" or "Use by" dates on shelf-stable and frozen packaged foods are relatively arbitrary.) "In short, I learned that selling fresh food wholesale is about the most difficult path you can take in the food world!" jokes Phil. "Nothing about it is easy." (To learn more about food safety and local regulations, check out the online classes offered by many universities and the official guidelines available at www.fda.gov.)

A Cook Made Good

When Phil moved into the larger, USDA-certified facility, growth became fast and furious—and Phil became a self-described "tornado of energy." Now that he had USDA certification, he could pitch and sell to larger, established stores: First the local Whole Foods and then Vitamin Cottage, a Western chain of natural food stores. "Suddenly, I was bringing in real revenue," says Phil. "And that's when I went from your normal sixty- to seventy-hour entrepreneurial workweek to this super crazy, self-abusive schedule." He was working 100 hours a week, week after week, month after month. His alarm clock went off at four in the morning and Phil would be running around until after midnight, squeezing in just a few hours of sleep a night.

Throughout 2002 and 2003, Phil's Fresh Foods was run 100 percent by, well, Phil. "I was cooking the eggs, I was doing the dishes, I was making deliveries," he says. He set up a system: On Monday, Wednesday, and Friday he'd call his customers and get his orders together. Then he'd grocery shop, go to the kitchen, and make burritos all day. As the evening crept by, he'd dive into the pile of dirty dishes he'd created, washing and sanitizing everything in sight. The next day—be it a Tuesday, Thursday, or Saturday— Phil would load up his van with coolers, icepacks, and burritos and go deliver, stocking refrigerator cases. And sometimes, on Sunday, he'd actually sleep for five or six hours.

But when Phil couldn't remember the last time he'd sneaked off for an afternoon of rock climbing, he knew he needed to hire some help. Phil had always thought of himself as just a cook, but he'd morphed into an entrepreneur too—and he could *hire* cooks. So he brought on kitchen staff, people who began working side by side with him. Some of those first employees still work for Phil today, although they've grown from cooks in jeans and backward baseball caps to supervisors with official training, hard hats, and uniforms! Phil also "hired" one more employee—a delivery driver who happened to be his girlfriend (and later, wife and business partner), Deborah. "I dragged her into my entrepreneurial madness," explains Phil. "And like the kitchen workers, her role grew as the company grew. We like to say she went from delivery driver to national sales manager!"

Go Frozen, Young Man

Phil kept building his business burrito by burrito: Phil's Fresh Foods expanded nationally, with his namesake line in Whole Foods and a private label collaboration with Wild Oats. But by 2007, Phil came to the single realization that would dramatically change the course of his business: The fresh wholesale model was not truly scalable. The food safety costs, distribution issues, and shelf-life mandates were limiting the volume and revenues Phil's Fresh Foods could ever hope to achieve.

By now, Phil had been in the burrito business for six years and finally felt like he knew his way around the food industry. For the first time, he understood why some brands were succeeding and others weren't, and he could look at the marketplace holistically. And that's when Phil realized his future wasn't in fresh foods; it was in the freezer aisle. Chipotle had expanded across the country and people were accustomed to the idea that burritos weren't just "cheap belly fill—they could be made with good-for-you ingredients and sophisticated flavors," says Phil. He connected the dots and this time he did consciously see the massive gap in the marketplace: a hole he could fill with premium, frozen convenience food, made with the same natural ingredients that were such a hit for Phil's Fresh Foods and Chipotle.

"I needed to rip the Band-Aid off," says Phil. "Fresh food felt safe because it was what I knew, but it wasn't the future of my brand." He'd been experimenting with frozen burritos for a few years, trying to create something that would taste just as good as a fresh one when heated. His main problem was mush: every filling would become reminiscent of baby food upon reheating. Finally, Phil figured out that he had to individually quick freeze (IQF) the burritos and calibrate an optimum level of moisture; together, those methods conquered the mush problem.

By early 2008, Phil was ready to launch a frozen line, which he introduced at the Natural Products Expo West in Anaheim, California. The frozen burritos were a hit! For the first time, mainstream distributors picked them up for national sales. Soon, retailers across the country started placing orders in amounts Phil had never seen before. Within months, Phil told his old accounts that he was switching completely over to frozen, and most were happy to take his new product. By 2009, Phil's Fresh Foods sold exclusively frozen burritos.

But this apparent success brought to light a fact Phil had spent years avoiding: the financial side of the business was in chaos. He woke up one morning with a chilling thought: "All of these people work for me and my credit cards are maxed out. How are we going to get through today, let alone grow?" Until then, the company's financing had consisted of cash flow coming in from revenues or racking up debt on Phil's credit cards. "It was financially reckless, and I couldn't support it anymore," remembers Phil.

So for the first time, Phil put his ideas down on paper, wrote a business plan, and went out to raise money. He was selling his new direction: Frozen food is the future. He raised about $200,000, mostly through friends and family—an amount which, at the time, panicked him. "What if I couldn't manage this huge sum of money?" says Phil. But in retrospect, he was already selling $2 million worth of burritos a year before he took a cent of financing. That $200,000 was nothing compared to what he had already built.

"If I were to go out today and tell an investor I wanted to build a frozen food factory with a $2 million a year capacity, they would say I'd need to start with at least $2 million," says Phil. "But I'd inadvertently, from a grassroots level, figured out how to run this company for just a tenth of that." That's part of the reason Phil was spread so thin: The company had no corporate employees. Phil and Deborah did everything—ordering, billing, sales, marketing, accounting, public relations—themselves. And, of course, that relatively small infusion of capital didn't go far. Phil realized that if he wanted to take Phil's Fresh Foods to the next level, he would need both significant financial help and significant guidance.

Howdy, Partners

Phil had a vision, energy, and manufacturing know-how. But he needed help figuring out finances, branding, and sales to really grow. He wrote a new version of his business plan to proclaim a new message: "Frozen burritos are working. Everyone loves them. There's a gap in the market. I think this thing can be big."

Phil wanted a $1 million infusion of capital. His thought was that if he could get his hands on that pie-in-the-sky amount, he could become a huge company. Phil got ready to make some big asks. For years, he'd been either locked in his plant making burritos or out on the streets selling them, wearing his trademark casual jeans and a T-shirt. Now he put on a suit and tie and began to play the networking game. Over the next year he met with more than seventy-five investors, always feeling like the proverbial fish out of water. Phil was wildly enthusiastic—and completely lacked the jargon and skill sets needed to sell an investment. After he'd talked to what felt like "everyone on the planet" he came to the conclusion that no one was about to write a $1 million check. So when a college buddy pointed Phil in the direction of Tom Spier, the former COO of Bear Naked granola, he was dubious.

He and Tom set up a meeting, even though Phil's expectations were sea-level low. But it took all of ten minutes for Phil's brain to start reeling with exclamation points: "The chemistry was so positive! Tom's vision for Phil's Fresh Foods was so enlightening! Here was a successful food entrepreneur who was young like me! Light bulbs were turning on everywhere!"

Phil was just as enthused when he met Tom's business partner, Brendan Synnott, who had cofounded Bear Naked. "They had the knowledge, wisdom, and capital that I didn't have," says Phil. "And I think they saw a fighter in me." And so a partnership was born: Tom was the finance guy, Brendan was the branding guy, and Phil was the food guy.

Over the next six months, they negotiated and prepped their deal. Tom and Brendan created a new corporation solely for the purpose of investing in Phil's Fresh Foods, called BIG (Burrito Investment Group). They and other investors then put money into BIG, and BIG in turn put the money into Phil's business for a stake of the equity. "A lot of people cautioned me that Tom and Brendan could effectively take over the business and push me out," says Phil. "And while that's true, I'm proud to say that four years later we have a great relationship, and I'm still here running things. But it was definitely nerve-wracking."

In March 2009, just when Phil had stretched his credit as far as it could possibly go, the first installment of investment money was wired into his account. Overnight, his worldview changed dramatically. "I had been operating with no budget, no capital, and no employees, and then we got proper capitalization," says Phil. The three new partners were ready to do something big, and fast. It was time to get to work.

The Launch of Evol

Part of that rapid growth meant that Phil's Fresh Foods was to be no more—at least in name. Tom and Brendan had been adamant during early negotiations that new branding was needed if they were going to take the business to the next level. It was completely fine with Phil: "If they thought there was another name that would help us get to the gold, then I was all for it," he says.

Just a few days after their deal was signed, Brendan called Phil early one morning. "Hey, I have the brand," he said.

"So you have some options?" asked Phil, assuming that this was going to be the start of a long process.

"No. Just one name," replied his partner. "I was thinking about the word *love* and wrote it in reverse, and then I flipped the *e* backwards."

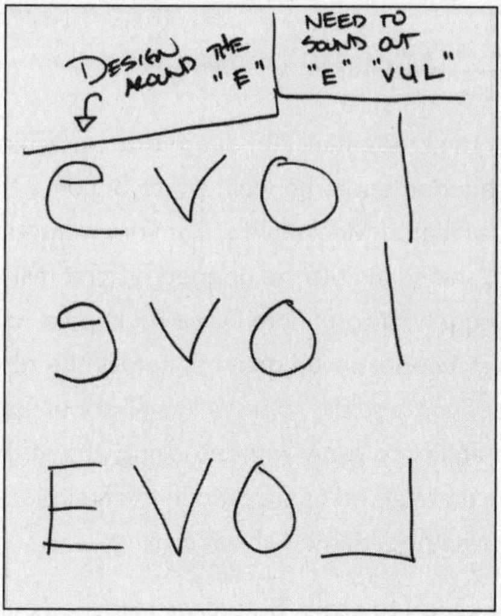

Courtesy Evol

Brainstorming the Evol name

The first time Phil's Fresh Foods was named, it had taken all of thirty seconds. Would this be just as fast?

"I didn't know how to react, because there was no logo or visual associated with this new name. It was just an amorphous concept," says Phil. Instead, he ventured, "All right . . . I think it's cool." But as he thought about it more, the idea grew on him. And when an artist took the idea and turned it into a real logo, Phil had to agree that it was hip and, yes, fresh. By the time they launched, he was in love with it.

At the time of the rebranding, Phil's Fresh Foods was selling $2 million worth of burritos a year in over 400 stores. How were they going to just switch their name overnight, while keeping their loyal followers? First, they went out to their customers, the grocery chain buyers, and explained the rebranding and Evol concept to each one: Evol equaled *love*, and *love* meant more than "Phil's."

SCALING UP LIKE A PRO

Tom Ryan's foodie credentials run deep: After inventing Pizza Hut's stuffed crust phenomenon, he went on to become the worldwide chief concept officer at McDonald's. But Tom wanted to give burgers soul again, and so in 2007 he opened his first fast-casual dining spot Smashburger with cofounder David Prokupek. Today, there are 170 locations in twenty-seven markets across the globe. How has Smashburger become so big so fast? "It's all about scalability," says Tom. "It's the ability to grow without losing any of the identifying characteristics that helped us succeed in the first place." Here, Tom shares the secrets he's learned about scaling:

1. Start with a vision to scale. Before we launched our first real restaurant, we spent six months in a test kitchen, figuring out our plan and creating a "kitchen engine" that was efficient and fast. The kitchen engine is the platform and process, which we then combine with people. For example, we have very modular surfaces in our kitchens. Our main piece of equipment is a griddle with a refrigerated area underneath filled with meatballs. It's the same at every location, and workers can grab what they need without leaving the grill. Then our whole process is high performance: We smash our burgers with a special cutter and technique, which means we can make a fresh burger, from scratch, in three minutes (a traditional burger can take eight). The systematic approach makes it easy to train and manage people and means we can open a new location without having to redesign each part from scratch.

2. Avoid the big brand or chain stigma by keeping a local focus. As you grow and expand, customers can see you as cookie cutter and lose interest. We fight that assumption by creating a local, aggressively marketed burger for each city, like the Colorado burger with roasted green chiles or the Miami burger with grilled chorizo.

We also find the best brew place in town and feature their beers exclusively. When we bring in area bloggers and media for a local beer and burger tasting event, people begin to think of us as a homegrown spot.

3. Be interesting, but simple. For example, our burger technique makes us different: We use bowl-chopped Angus meat—thin slices that have never been squeezed—instead of ground beef for a unique burger flavor. That and our local burgers and brews help differentiate us from other fast-casual and burger spots, but they're also simple, regimented, and easy to reproduce.

"The Phil's name and logo was everything I needed in the beginning—crunchy, hippie-dippy, farmers' markety," explains Phil. "But the new logo and name gave us a clean, premium vibe. It's what we needed to expand the company."

Phil's Fresh Foods already had national distribution before the rebranding, but just in the *natural channel,* which includes stores like Whole Foods, Sprouts Farmers Market, and Vitamin Cottage. The Evol trio's goal was to quickly get into the *grocery channel*, which includes places like Kroger, SuperValu, and Safeway. But even that wasn't straightforward. The grocery channel is further divided into a *natural section* and a *main-line section*, which operate as almost entirely separate entities. Evol had to clarify that they wanted to be in the natural section of grocery, next to Amy's and Kashi. (A spot in main-line grocery would make Evol compete with brands like Stouffer's and Lean Cuisine, products with lower price points and a different type of appeal.)

So when Evol officially launched in August 2009, its products were sold in both the natural and the grocery channels for the first time, a move that vastly expanded their market. From day one, they were in 1,000 stores, and the number grew rapidly. Within a year, Evol was sold in 4,000 stores. (Today, Phil estimates that Evol can be found in at least 7,000 stores.)

Beyond the Burrito

As Phil, Tom, and Brendan reworked their business plan throughout 2009, they began to look beyond their successful burrito line. "We have unique ownership over this concept of 'love, premium, and frozen,' which we believe transcends grocery store categories," says Phil. Could Evol become a multicategory brand? Their strategic goal was to move from the Handheld category—burritos, frozen sandwiches, pockets, egg rolls, samosas, quesadillas, tacos—to the much larger Meal category. "It seemed like a logical stepping-stone," says Phil, "and it's been wildly successful." The plan is to eventually expand into other categories, especially snacks. Now the management team thinks about Evol in terms of four categories—Handheld, Meal, Pizzas, and Snacks—each with the potential to be huge.

Today, Evol has a revolving cast of approximately thirty-five products in their collection, but they're constantly adding new ones and swapping out underperformers. But it's not just hit-and-miss guesswork; part of the financial and operational overhaul means that Phil can now analyze up-to-the-minute data on almost any aspect of the company. He has a number of computer dashboards that let him see everything from how much Evol is spending on a customer, how much they're shipping to a store, the return on marketing efforts, and exactly what products are selling, sorted further by things like natural channel, grocery channel, and geographic location.

Evol also purchases data (from places like Nielsen and IRI) to help evaluate both its sales and general food retail trends. "Any time we introduce a new product, we first have to understand what's happening in the market, and then overlap that with our innovation strategy," says Phil. For example, three years ago, their strategy was to "win" the natural channel and simply overflow into grocery. To do that, they developed product flavors that they thought would win the hearts and minds of both natural channel store buyers and consumers, without worrying if the products would have more mainstream, grocery channel appeal. At one point, they were making a hundred different products! But now that they're on solid ground in natural, Evol is focusing on grocery and products that can do well across both channels.

Phil also loves analyzing regional preferences for flavors, types of items, and sizes. For example, Evol's egg and green chile breakfast burrito is the number one selling natural burrito in Colorado. That's an amazing data point because it doesn't exist anywhere else in the United States. "If we were to put egg and green chile on the shelf in New York City, it would not move. If we were to put egg and green chile in Florida, it would not move," says Phil. But in Colorado, land of green chile lovers, it works. On a similar note, their pork green chile burrito is a hit in natural but was a nonstarter in grocery. "Sometimes people say, 'I wish you guys would push the envelope more,'" says Phil. "And we try to, but at the end of the day it's our chicken, bean and rice, and shredded beef-types of products that consumers actually *buy.* They might not appeal to the ultra-foodies, but they're more inclusive and do well for us nationally."

So these days, when Phil wants to create a new product, he doesn't just head into the kitchen and start cooking. First, there's research: What do the natural and grocery channel stores actually *need* on their shelves? If they need the product—or if Evol can explain why they need it—buyers are more likely to say yes. Then, once the new product is ready, the marketing team comes in to create a story: "Here's why this product exists. Here's why it benefits consumers. Here's why you, as a retailer, should carry it." Finally, the sales team takes that narrative to retailers, tailoring the message to each store or buyer's needs. And, they hope, buyers stock it and consumers buy it!

In between, of course, there are a thousand other steps, such as actually cooking and manufacturing the product, calculating sustainable profit margins, making sure that the product's nutritional stats are reasonable, and keeping everything in line with the Evol branding. But the short process is to innovate based on what the market needs, create a marketing story, sell the innovation to the retailer, and promote the new product when it's on the shelves. "After a lot of organizational work, that's how we now operate," explains Phil. "It's clean, data driven, and measurable."

So, You Want to Be Like Phil?

Today, Phil is living in what he calls the "Golden Age of Evol." "We're a multimillion-dollar brand, we've experienced massive growth and we're continuing to experience massive growth, and we have an amazing team. Now my goal is simply to enjoy the journey," he says. And for the first time in years, he's back outside in the Boulder foothills. (Although these days, Phil is more likely to be found taking his young children for a wilderness hike than scaling epic cliffs.) And only occasionally does he put in 100-hour workweeks.

For those who dream of their own golden age someday, Phil says that his first, and most important, piece of advice is to clearly articulate why you want to be an entrepreneur. Do you want to be rich? Do you love being in the kitchen all day? Do you want to change the way the majority of America eats? Do you want to support a small, artisan farmer, bread maker, or chocolatier? There are many, many answers; the important thing is knowing what *your* answer is.

"The reasons I got up every day eleven years ago are very different from what motivates me now," says Phil. "It took me a long time before I had a mission and understood the higher purpose of this business. In 2001, I wanted to be an entrepreneur because I was sick of taking orders and answering to other people. I wanted to rock climb every day. And to be honest, I probably wanted to prove something to myself and to the world. But I think it's extremely rare that someone who pursues a business the way I did, in a rather haphazard way with no clear vision, will be successful. Sometimes I feel like it's all a bit miraculous.

"Be optimistic, but also humble and realistic. Everything is going to take twice as long as you think it will. It's going to cost twice as much and it's going to cause five times more brain damage than you ever thought possible." Phil pauses, then laughs. "I think entrepreneurs constantly tell themselves it's going to get easier. It doesn't get easier, but it does keep getting more and more fun."

TAKE AWAY

- **Prepare for a labyrinth of regulations.** You'll probably need to work in a certified facility unless your product falls under "cottage laws," which vary by state; sometimes, small-batch baked goods like cookies can be made at home. Otherwise, culinary schools, small-business associations, and local food entrepreneurs should be able to direct you to commercial kitchen space. Then you'll have to undergo shelf-life and safety testing and defend your methods to the USDA and FDA, depending on the product. Learn more at the online classes offered by many universities and the official guidelines available at www.fda.gov.

- **When it comes to safety, not all food products are equal.** Different foods require different levels of regulation. In general, anything that's fresh, contains meat, or is sold wholesale requires more specialized, expensive, and extensive certification than do products that are shelf stable, are sold directly to consumers, or are plant based. For example, Phil learned that selling fresh, meat-containing food wholesale is exponentially more regulated than, say, selling cookies.

- **Some products scale better than others.** Phil found that food safety costs and distribution issues made it difficult to scale the fresh wholesale model. Moving into the frozen sector reduced those costs while dramatically increasing the time his items could remain on a store's shelves and widening his distribution reach. If you want to scale a business, look for a nonperishable product that can be shipped far and wide or create a platform and product that can easily be replicated in various locations, like the Smashburger kitchen engines.

5

Navigating the World of Manufacturing

MARY'S GONE CRACKERS

Long before gluten-free *became a buzzword, Mary Waldner was making wholesome, addictive crackers that fit her celiac disease lifestyle. Today she's making them for a gluten-free world.*

A Life-Changing Diagnosis

Imagine feeling sick—not for a day, or a week, or even a year, but for your whole life. That was reality for Mary Waldner, who, by the age of three, was regularly experiencing painful digestion after meals.

Today, the sixty-two-year-old marriage and family therapist from northern California still acutely remembers the agony she felt as a child. "My earliest memories are of my mother rocking me to sleep as I cried, because the pain in my stomach was so overwhelming," she says. As Mary got older, the symptoms only worsened, leaving her fatigued and suffering from constant, low-level depression. While she had a hunch that her ailment was food related, she had no idea what

Courtesy Mary's Gone Crackers

Mary Waldner in the Mary's Gone Crackers factory

was causing it. Worse, doctors seemed to think her pain was all in her head.

Mary tried everything throughout the 1980s and 1990s—allergy shots, holistic doctors, special diets—but to no avail. By then Mary had a thriving therapy practice and was married with a young son, but her unnamed, undiagnosed illness was taking over her life.

Finally, in 1994, when she was forty-three years old, Mary's chiropractor came up with a possible diagnosis. Could it be a little-known disease called celiac? (Of course, fast-forwarding to the present, celiac disease awareness has risen so dramatically that it would be one of the very first things a doctor might test for! But when Mary first heard of it, the term was completely foreign to her and a large majority of

Americans.) The condition is an autoimmune disease that damages the intestines when gluten (a natural substance found in wheat, rye, and barley that gives bread and baked goods their beloved elastic qualities) is consumed. The result is bloating, diarrhea, and malabsorption of nutrients, which leads to fatigue, anemia, and myriad other illnesses. This could explain why Mary constantly felt sick; her body had been fighting off poisonous invaders for decades.

The only true test for the disease, however, was for Mary to give up gluten entirely for at least a month and monitor her symptoms. She switched to the new diet and started to feel better almost immediately; within thirty days, it was a "night and day difference," she says. "The change in how I both felt and looked was so dramatic that I'd run into friends I hadn't seen for a while, and they would barely recognize me. I looked like I was at least ten years younger, and I had energy I'd never had before!"

Mary was so thrilled to have a diagnosis—and a solution—that throwing out all of her bread, crackers, and gluten-containing grains was almost a celebration. "If I felt better, I didn't care a bit if I could never have a piece of bread again," she says. But it wasn't like her culinary options went to zero: Mary had long been an avid baker and promptly started playing with gluten-free grains and flours, like brown rice and quinoa. "It was like a whole new world had opened up for me," she remembers. "Suddenly, I was thinking outside of the wheat box. Could food be my medicine?"

From Celiac to Crackers

As Mary adapted to her new dietary lifestyle during the mid-1990s, she was going at it alone. "I didn't know anybody else who was avoiding gluten, and I didn't meet a single other celiac patient until years later," she says. "There weren't Internet support groups and whole websites dedicated to celiac and gluten intolerance like there are today. My son, who was nine at the time, had the same issues, so it was the two of us." At home, Mary could control their food fairly easily, but with her newfound energy and enthusiasm, she wanted to go out and socialize!

She devised strategies for avoiding gluten in social situations, always volunteering to bring dessert and something else she could eat. Often, she would bring two or three whole dishes to any potluck or dinner party. She didn't mind at all because she was just so happy to feel better. And while most people might not have understood what a gluten-free diet was, they enjoyed the delicious food Mary was serving.

Dining out at restaurants, however, was another issue—especially when it came to the omnipresent bread. In contrast to circulating, drink in hand, at someone's home before dinner, restaurant dining trapped Mary at the table, with only a big basket of gluten in sight. "It was one of the hardest situations," she says. "While everyone else was munching on warm, fluffy slices, I was starving and couldn't eat anything."

While she wasn't consciously looking for a fix, Mary started playing with an idea for a predinner snack. On a quiet Sunday in 1995, she combined brown rice, quinoa, flaxseeds, and sesame seeds by hand, cutting the baked results into crispy, cracker-like pieces. They were good. Really good. That week, Mary made another batch, and then another. As she tweaked her recipe, Mary realized that these crunchy, portable snacks were crackers; she'd concocted a gluten-free cracker! From then on, Mary kept a stash at work, brought bags to parties, and munched on them in lieu of raiding the bread basket.

The crackers were a big hit everywhere she went. It had nothing to do with their gluten-free properties; at the time, nobody knew or cared about that. But across the board, people loved them. "I'd watch kids, teenagers, and their parents gobble them up," says Mary. "Both the health-conscious vegetarians and the friends who ate cheeseburgers daily would exclaim how delicious they were." And she began to think that there might be something extraordinary about these crackers.

Mary's friends offered her their utmost culinary praise: "You should write a cookbook!" While Mary could see where they were coming from, her recipe was both difficult and time intensive. In fact, even when she gave people her step-by-step directions, they never made the crackers because the process took at least five hours and was ridiculously messy. Who wouldn't rather have their friend Mary just bring a batch to a party?

And then, on the morning of January 1, 1999, after a holiday fete where hundreds of her crackers had been snapped up, Mary awoke with a flash of an idea: She should manufacture and *sell* the crackers. She immediately told her husband, Dale Rodrigues, about her brainstorm. Could they do it? Dale readily agreed, even though it was the first time either had even considered this crazy proposition.

But if the crackers were next-to-impossible to make at home, then people would be willing to pay for them, right? The idea for Mary's Gone Crackers was officially born. It would be five years before Mary launched her line into grocery stores, and by then she would have made an estimated 30,000 crackers by hand in her home kitchen. But now she knew where she—and her passion for gluten-free—were headed.

Jumping into Business

For the next few years, Mary and Dale continued their full-time jobs—she as a therapist, he as a general contractor—while filling every second of free time with cracker research and planning. Mary's role was to find the right equipment and figure out how to transition her handmade recipe into something more automated, while Dale would handle the finances and write a business plan.

To set their scheme in motion they first needed a name, but nothing was sticking. Would their venture end for lack of moniker? Mary was venting about the challenge to her women's therapist group when one of the members said, "I think your name should be in it, like Mary's Crackin' Up." Another friend exclaimed, "Mary's Gone Crackers!" "It was like the sky opened up and the angels sang. That was it," says Mary. (And yes, Mary's friend still takes great pride in the fact that she came up with the name!)

In 2002, another hurdle surfaced: money. When Mary significantly reduced her workload and Dale left his job, they quickly began racking up scary credit card debt. The only way they could make peace with the risk was their faith that they would eventually be successful; after all, they'd seen more over-the-top enthusiastic reactions to the crackers than they could count. Although it wouldn't be fun, they calculated that they could repay all of their growing debt within four years. And so, with their strong faith intact, they turned the business into their (unpaid) full-time jobs.

Gluten-Free or Bust

Manufacturing a new food product is challenging under any circumstances, let alone when attempting to do it with an entirely new way of baking! While few people had heard of gluten-free circa 2003, even fewer had ever attempted to make gluten-free products. There were no guides for Mary to follow, and no one to ask for advice; she'd have to invent the wheel herself.

Mary's first forays took her to a bakery equipment supply store, but most of the standard items relied on the natural elasticity of gluten. So she broadened her search and looked far outside of the food industry. She eventually even repurposed a machine typically used in the cosmetics industry! While it was a struggle at the time, today Mary recognizes it as lucky; because she invented so much of the Mary's Gone Crackers process from scratch, it's that much harder for competitors to copy what she's doing.

As they researched, Dale thought that he and Mary should put their new knowledge to use and open up their own factory. Mary, however, advocated for using a co-packer, who would make the crackers to their specifications. "I'd argue that we weren't manufacturers and didn't know nearly enough to run our own factory," remembers Mary. Dale retorted, "Find me a truly gluten-free facility, one that's willing to work with an entirely new type of product, and I'll agree with you." He had a point. It was going to be a tough order to fill.

Mary found a book that listed all of the co-packers in the United States (today, directories are often electronic). It included the kinds of things they made and the basic equipment they had on site. When she didn't find a single co-packer who fit their needs, Mary got creative. She went into her kitchen and pulled out every gluten-free product she had (not that there were many on the market to choose from). Then she picked up the phone and called the company who made each item, working her way through the hierarchy until she found someone to answer two questions: Who were their co-packers? Or would they manufacture her product? The answers were less than heartening.

Then Mary picked up a frozen pizza crust from a little company in Chico, California, and finally got her big break. She reached the owner, explained her dilemma, and asked if they'd be able to make her crackers. For the first time, the answer was yes! "It seemed like a miracle," says Mary. "If it weren't for them, we'd never have gotten started."

Mary drove up to their facility and began to refine her formula for this new, automated equipment. "I was obviously very attached to keeping the recipe as close to my original as possible," she says. "But the dough kept coming out much too dry." The two women who owned the place wanted to add more water, but Mary was afraid that such a significant change would undo the alchemy of her carefully calibrated process.

To calm her fears, they decided to do a blind taste test: the machine-made crackers with more water versus Mary's original handmade crackers. "Lo and behold, everyone liked the new version better!" says Mary. While the texture was slightly different, it was something Mary could accept. And as an unexpected bonus, the crackers were sturdier and less prone to breaking. All in all, by the end of 2004, Mary had devised a machine-made cracker she liked even more than her homemade ones.

Even with a co-packer and a working recipe, manufacturing the crackers still turned out to be a full-time job. "I'd had this vague idea that we would run everything from afar," says Mary. "But co-packing does not mean outsourcing!" She and Dale began commuting the three hours between the Bay Area and Chico multiple times a week. And although they were grateful for the space and introduction to manufacturing that the little pizza crust company had given them, its workers and facility weren't set up to meet the high volume or quality standards that Mary wanted.

In retrospect, Mary wishes she'd had more conversations with their co-packer upfront. "I should have specified the standards, raw materials, and features that were most important to me," she explains. She also wishes they'd had a stronger contract that clearly laid out expectations for the finished products ("specs"), along with the legal and financial ramifications of not meeting them.

So after a few months, Mary's Gone Crackers negotiated a solution and took over production of their own product within the other company's facility. Dale used all of the skills he'd picked up as a general contractor and spent two weeks interviewing candidates, and then overnight they went from having one employee to twenty. And for the next year and a half, as Mary's Gone Crackers went from a dream to a national success, they continued to operate out of that pizza crust factory. But their next step was clear; soon, they'd need their own, much larger, facility.

Going Crackers

In the beginning, Mary and Dale thought they knew exactly who their target market was: the celiac population. After all, in 2004 and 2005, those were the only people interested in gluten-free. But whenever they told a food industry veteran about their idea, the advice was the same: don't put *gluten-free* on your package! The theory was that it would make the product seem medicinal and not for normal, everyday

SPECIAL DIETARY NEED? THERE'S A MARKET FOR THAT

Nineteen years ago, when Mary's chiropractor first broached the idea of celiac disease, she had never even heard of the term *gluten*, let alone been able to buy a host of products made just for her needs. The special dietary needs market—which includes wheat- and gluten-free, peanut-free, tree nut–free, soy-free, dairy-free, egg-free, and shellfish-free (90 percent of food allergies in the United States are attributed to these foods)—has changed dramatically since then. In fact, Mary and Dale never imagined that food allergy and intolerance awareness would become the considerable dietary and social movement it is now.

Until the early 2000s, celiac disease (and by extension, any degree of gluten intolerance) was a little-known phenomenon. As late as 1999, medical textbooks reported that the incidence of celiac disease was 1 in 10,000 people and that rates were declining. But Italian doctor Alessio Fasano didn't believe it. He undertook the first large-scale study ever done on celiac disease in the United States and in 2003 published results suggesting that 1 in every 133 Americans had celiac.

But the medical breakthroughs would take years to trickle down to the average consumer. When Mary and Dale started making their crackers in 2004 and 2005, there were just a handful of companies focusing on gluten-free (as opposed to the thousands that do so today). And awareness was minimal: The common response when people heard about Mary's diet was, "What's gluten?" Even the companies that were making gluten-free products weren't using certified gluten-free facilities; there wasn't a sizable market for them, so they simply didn't exist.

It's now estimated that 18 million Americans have some degree of gluten sensitivity, and most know what the gluten-free label on

Mary's Gone Crackers packages means. The demand is still growing: By comparing blood samples from the 1950s to today, Dr. Fasano found that modern teenagers are five times as likely to have celiac disease. In 2011, the research firm Spin Group reported that the gluten-free market was a $6.3 billion industry, and one poised for even more rapid growth. As with any quickly growing industry, federal regulations and guidelines are just now getting under way, with proposed limits for a certified gluten-free label. Meanwhile, a nonprofit, the Gluten-Free Certification Organization, manages the most-recognized third-party certification and audits (gfco.org).

Similar research and understanding has occurred with other common allergens: for example, it's now estimated that 1.5 percent of the population has a peanut allergy.

These other special-needs diets are also experiencing tremendous growth: Approximately 15 million Americans have diagnosed food allergies (a number that doesn't include gluten or dairy allergies or intolerances, like lactose intolerance). In a crowded grocery store market, they make up a brand new, not-so-niche category known as *free-from*.

consumption. But Mary decided that if she were the customer, she'd want to know, so she put small *wheat-free* and *gluten-free* designations on the box. "We didn't make it a big, flashy thing like brands do now," she says, "but if people were looking for gluten-free then they would find the label. And if they weren't looking for gluten-free, then they could just ignore it."

Dale discovered that there were over 400 celiac support groups across the country, and Mary's Gone Crackers sent samples to every single one of them. They also targeted an online store, the Gluten-Free Mall, as the perfect place to sell their first products. But to get in the mall, they had to be accepted by its distributor. Luckily, the small, Pennsylvania-based distributor agreed to take them on. (Distributors usually don't want to carry a product unless it's already in distribution, a complete catch-22 situation.)

Slowly but surely, Mary's Gone Crackers were picked up by more local distributors and started getting into small, independent stores. Mary would load the truck drivers up with samples, which they'd then drop off with each delivery they made. Soon, store managers across the East Coast were snacking on Mary's crackers.

While Mary and Dale were pouring energy into their grassroots efforts, they learned that the ultimate goal of many small food companies was to get picked up by the large, powerful distributor UNFI (United Natural Foods Inc.). So they filled out the application, sent in the required samples, and then took it one step further. They found a list of the 100 highest-grossing natural food stores and sent a box of their crackers, along with a personalized cover letter, to each and every one. "Our sole marketing strategy was to get our crackers into people's mouths," says Mary. "We were sure that once someone tried our crackers, they would want to carry them."

Then all Mary and Dale could do was wait and hope for good news. Mary was going through a stack of mail a few months later when she saw a thin envelope from UNFI and her stomach sank; just like with college admissions letters, thin probably meant bad news. Sure enough, it was a standard, one-sheet rejection note. But when Mary moved on to the next piece of mail in her pile, she found some entirely different news.

It seemed that the buyer for a large Pacific Northwest chain had loved the sample crackers Mary had sent. The buyer had called UNFI and asked them to carry Mary's Gone Crackers because she wanted to stock them. "And her stores were such a big customer for UNFI that they immediately agreed!" exclaims Mary. "Somehow, we received our acceptance letter and our rejection letter on the same day!" Now almost any grocery store in the United States could ask for Mary's Gone Crackers and have them simply and easily delivered. And soon, unbeknown to Mary and Dale, *gluten-free* would become a buzzword—and Mary's crackers were now perfectly primed to reach millions of new consumers across the country.

Gluten-Free Meets Venture Capital

It seems as if Mary and Dale had the perfect product for the zeitgeist of the moment. Had they reached easy, cruising altitude? Not in the least; they were about to go through their most challenging entrepreneurial experience yet. Although the couple hadn't forecasted the rise of gluten-free or the mainstream appeal of their crackers, industry experts and investors were soon eyeing the potential of the brand and encouraging Mary and Dale to expand.

That factory they'd been meaning to open for years? It was time. But to do that, they needed to raise a large amount of money, and quickly. Investment dollars seemed to appear out of nowhere, but Mary and Dale also made sure to put a significant chunk of their own money into the pot. Dale's mother had died, and he was adamant that his inheritance be spent on the company. "Otherwise, we would lose our percentage of ownership," he explains. "The more money you take from other people, the less you own of your company."

The very first time they took outside money, in 2004, Mary and Dale kept an ownership stake of 65 percent. They knew that 51 percent was the magic number, but over the years as they took more money, which they needed to fund their rapid growth, their ownership percentage became diluted. "If we had not put our own money in repeatedly, we would probably own just 6 or 7 percent of the company now," says Mary. (Throughout this general period they owned 26 percent.) "It turns out that even when we thought we were being smart, we were incredibly naive and made some consequential mistakes."

Those mistakes started building when they moved into their new factory in 2006 and demand for their crackers kept rising. "That always sounds like a great thing. The higher the demand, the more you sell, the more cash you make, right? Yes, it's great, but it also brings huge problems," says Mary. In the grocery business you send inventory out to stores, but you don't get cash payment for those goods (the accounts receivable) right away. Instead, there's a *floating inventory* that can easily run into a million dollars: goods you've made and delivered (and paid upfront for the labor and ingredients) but haven't yet received payment for. The problem arises when all of a company's cash is tied up in floating inventory and it needs more cash to continue daily operations, like purchasing ingredients and paying salaries.

Mary and Dale were caught up in a whirlwind of cash flow issues when they were approached by a venture capital group. Their first instinct was to be honored . . . and relieved. *Venture capital* (VC) refers to private money that funds high-growth, high-potential companies in exchange for equity, but without a regulated, stock market–type public offering. Mary and Dale had met some of the members previously at food shows and were thrilled they had been tapped for partnership. Here was the crucial cash they needed, from people they trusted.

The capital infusion was critical to their rocket-speed growth, but Mary and Dale hadn't anticipated the full effects of bringing on this type of partner. "Their agenda was to quickly grow our company," Mary says, "and prepare it for sale, regardless of whether or not we

HOW TO GET A GREAT MENTOR

Janie Hoffman, the founder of Mamma Chia beverages, got a little help from her favorite mentors—Mary and Dale, from Mary's Gone Crackers. Here, Janie talks about how she created and nurtured the relationship.

1. Bond over common interests first. I met Mary at a Slow Money conference, and we talked for ages about our mutual love of tiny, omega-3-packed chia seeds. Not too many people knew about them, but I wanted to put them in a beverage and Mary was already using them in her products.

2. Ask to make the relationship official. When Mary invited me to a Christmas party, I decided to just ask if she and Dale would mentor me as I tried to navigate the world of a start-up business. They were thrilled to do so, and now they're my source for straightforward advice as well as general encouragement.

3. Trust your mentor's instincts. A lot of folks in the industry said that our product was too weird (gelatinous chia seeds are suspended throughout a lightly sweetened drink). But Mary, like me, thought that chia seeds were going to be big. And sure enough, Mamma Chia became one of the top-selling beverages when it was introduced at Whole Foods, and then quickly crossed over into the mainstream grocery channel.

4. Value (and ask for) his or her connections and wisdom. Mary and Dale coached me through my Whole Foods approach, introduced me to our first distributor, and helped me avoid some of the financial challenges they'd faced. Plus they always remind me to stay sane and enjoy the ride. Mary asks me, "Are you doing yoga?" It's her way of reminding me to stay balanced.

wanted to sell it. And, unfortunately, we didn't understand that at the beginning. They encouraged us to rapidly expand. 'Don't worry about costs, just grow, grow, grow.' Then of course, we quickly and desperately needed more money. But with each infusion of capital, we lost a percentage of ownership."

Working with the venture capital group started to feel like a perilous balancing act; there were too many competing interests within Mary's Gone Crackers. Eventually, Mary and Dale realized that if they took much more VC money they would completely lose control of their company. So they made a conscious decision to change direction; they needed to be profitable, not high growth. They slowed their expansion and stopped taking on new accounts and launching product lines. Instead, they focused on maintaining a positive cash flow. Within three months, they recorded their first profits, and vowed never to take VC money again. And on December 31, 2012, they reached a deal that made everyone happy. All of their investors, including family and friends, sold their shares to the Japanese cracker company Kameda Seika. Mary and Dale retained a 20 percent share and what they wanted most—the ability to run their own company.

Mary Goes Cookies . . . and Beyond!

When Mary's Gone Crackers first moved from their co-packer's facility, a 7,500-square-foot spot they shared with another company, into their new 50,000-square-foot home in 2006, they didn't even know what to do with the space. "We used just a tiny corner of it," says Mary. "Everybody kept saying, 'Oh, you're going to outgrow this too.' I didn't believe them!" Sure enough, in 2012, she and Dale took over the adjacent 100,000-square-foot facility, and their 200 employees run machines 24/7.

In 2012, Mary's Gone Crackers also ramped up for their first national Costco deal. "Costco had wanted to work with us for a while, but we knew our capacity was too limited," explains Mary. "Finally, we reached a level where Dale knew we could create the crackers they needed for a big promotional push." To make it work, Mary's Gone Crackers *tripled* their production, and were in every Costco for the month of February. To pull it off, they bought more equipment and worked more hours, but they also became more efficient. "That's part of what expansion means for us now," says Mary. "Doing what we're already doing, but better."

Today, the Mary's Gone Crackers line also includes cookies, pretzels, and baking crumbs, all gluten-free, nut-free, vegan, and organic. They also pay attention to allergies like soy, scrupulously listing where and when they use certain ingredients and the possibility of cross-contamination. "My inspiration still comes from what I like to eat," says Mary. "And after struggling with my own dietary restrictions, I try to be sensitive to the restrictions of others—hence the nut-free, dairy-free viewpoint we take."

Mary and Dale still consider the crackers to be the engine to their train, the superstar that pulls all of their other products along. And even as the gluten-free marketplace exploded, the crackers became a true crossover product with mainstream appeal. Today, Mary's Gone Crackers is thinking about different packaging and uses for those crackers just as much as they're thinking about new lines. First up: getting the crackers into food service (like college and hospital cafeterias), on airlines, and into vending machines.

"People will talk to me all the time and say, 'Poor you; gluten-free must be so limiting and hard. How can you do it?' And while there are certainly moments when it's challenging, this lifestyle has opened up a whole world of amazing ingredients to me," exclaims Mary. "And it was the problem that led to the cracker solution which led to Mary's Gone Crackers." By now Mary has sold over 8 million boxes of those crackers, which can be found in 10,000 stores. All in all, not a bad result from a celiac diagnosis.

TAKE AWAY

- **Consider both opening your own facility and co-packing.** If your product involves special equipment or lots of labor, it might make sense to have a co-packer make it (instead of producing it yourself in a commercial kitchen or opening your own facility). Find one by looking at resources like Bevnet.com, SpecialtyFood.com, and necfe.foodscience.cornell.edu, or do an Internet search for "co-packer" + "[your state]".
- **Communicate with your co-packer.** Once you've visited and like a co-packer, have the tough conversations up front. Specify your standards for raw materials and dietary restrictions (for example, no nuts in the facility for a nut-free product) and the finished product (the specs) along with the legal and financial ramifications of not meeting them.
- **Co-packing does not mean hands-off!** In fact, it can still be a full-time job, especially while you finalize product development, packaging, and distribution. Don't expect to send in an order and check it off the list. And if other options fail, you might consider managing your own manufacturing in a co-packer's facility.

6

The Power of Equity

JUSTIN'S NUT BUTTERS

Justin Gold whips up crazy peanut butter flavors to fuel his active lifestyle; when his roommates keep swiping it, he realizes there might be a market for his homemade concoctions.

Go West, Young Man

Justin Gold's original life plan had nothing to do with nut butters and everything to do with the bestseller *A Civil Action*. The book, which recounts the travails of a crusading environmental lawyer, resonated with Justin, who sports an easygoing smile, a mop of curly hair, and surfer good looks. "I grew up in western Pennsylvania in an old mining and logging town," he explains. "And I was always outdoors hiking, climbing, and exploring. Nature was a big part of my life." The book inspired him to pursue a similar law career, but a legal internship left him completely disillusioned with the day-to-day reality of what it was like to be a lawyer. "It was, as anyone else would have guessed, very different from the movies!" he says, laughing.

Without a career beckoning, Justin instead moved west to Colorado as soon as he graduated from college in 2000. He waited tables

Todd Powers

Justin Gold with his nut butters

to pay the rent and spent the rest of his time hiking, running, and skiing. All of that activity left him in great shape—and very hungry. "I had become a vegetarian during college, when I learned about the environmental impact of eating meat," he explains. "But I still needed lots of energy to fuel my long outdoor treks." He did some research and found that one of the best sources of plant-based protein is nut butter. Soon, Justin was eating so much peanut and almond butter that he didn't even bother to put it on anything; he'd eat it straight out of the jar with a spoon. He would have some as a prehike meal, while watching a movie, or as a late-night snack. "It was my food of choice," he says, allowing that yes, he really, really likes nut butters. But within a few months, he was bored; there was no variety in the organic peanut butters he found at his local store. Man cannot live on plain peanut butter alone, apparently. On a whim he started stirring in toppings like chocolate chips, vanilla extract, and dried blueberries to spice things up a bit.

Justin was having so much fun with the combinations he was inventing—think vanilla birthday cake and blueberry–maple syrup—that he started wondering why no one was selling something like it. He'd be the first to buy a jar! And once that question had entered Justin's head, he unknowingly began the long road toward Justin's Nut Butters.

Next Stop: Peanut Butter

After it occurred to Justin that there might be a market for his concoctions, he considered what would be required. The first step alone seemed insurmountable: How do you even *make* peanut butter? A little investigation found that the iconic spread requires remarkably little magic. You take peanuts, put them in a food processor, let it run, and, voilà, peanut butter. "I started making my own, just to play," remembers Justin. While it was mixing, he'd add in things like honey, maple syrup, coconut flakes, strawberries, or chocolate, whatever sounded good. He was surprised to find that the results were better than the previous stir-in versions he'd made with store-bought nut butters and definitely worth the effort it took to make. He'd find an old jar, fill it with the homemade nut butter, and scrawl his name all over (oftentimes adding in a warning of "DO NOT TOUCH!"). The labeling was key; he was living with a bunch of roommates who would help themselves to whatever looked appetizing, and Justin's nut butters—

labeled or not—quickly became one of everyone's favorite foods. "At least by labeling it, I could *hope* they'd leave it alone," says Justin, laughing.

But in a fortuitous stroke, his roommates' love for the peanut butter was just the incentive Justin needed to think beyond his own personal snack food. The jars he stocked in the cupboard, with the handwritten *Justin's*, looked like the artisanal, small-batch products at the Boulder farmers' markets, and his roommates were soon encouraging Justin to set up a table there as well.

Justin discovered that he would need to make the butters in an FDA-approved facility, even if he was just selling a few jars at the market. Although some states now allow small producers to make certain food items out of their homes (generally cooked or baked goods like jams and muffins), Colorado didn't at the time. (To find out the regulations for your state, search for "cottage food laws.") And once Justin committed to making his nut butters in an authorized kitchen, he might as well think bigger. Could he sell to local stores too? That would mean he'd need a real label and all sorts of other "official" things he didn't have the first inkling of how to do.

So Justin took a trip to his neighborhood grocery store and found a section of locally made products. He wrote down the names and phone numbers of every area company he could find, places making salsas, relishes, and granola. Then Justin picked up the phone and started dialing, asking whether anyone would have ten or fifteen minutes to answer a few questions. The technique, with all of its grassroots, no-MBA-required appeal, worked remarkably well. "I was able to start networking and meeting entrepreneurs," says Justin. "And that ten minutes I asked for often led to much longer talks."

Smaller businesses in particular were remarkably willing to help.

For example, the owner of a salsa company went out of his way to explain both the big and the small stuff to Justin. While executives at larger companies couldn't sit down with some young start-up, established entrepreneurs who had worked through the same simple, but incredibly confusing, questions themselves became Justin's best resources. They gave him advice on everything from getting a Universal Product Code (UPC) to where to buy glass jars in bulk and print his labels. And because they were in the area, they could point Justin to the same local places and companies they'd used.

He hadn't yet made it to the farmers' market, but Justin was realizing that if he wanted to really pursue this nut butter scheme, he should get organized. First step: writing a business plan. His growing network of fellow food entrepreneurs referred him to two resources: the Small Business Development Center, a hub for local business where Justin took a $75 afternoon course in business-plan writing and met with an adviser; and Colorado University's business library. It turned out that anyone, student or not, could use the library resources. "It was like stumbling on a gold mine of free information!" exclaims Justin. "I spent weeks just thumbing through their business books and learning everything I could."

Justin wrote his first business plan during the fall of 2002, all the while continuing to wait tables to support himself. When his plan—thirty pages detailing everything from manufacturing, branding, pricing, marketing, and financing—was ready, he went to family members and friends and explained what he wanted to do. He raised about $150,000, added in his own life savings, and Justin's Nut Butters was ready to go live.

And They Said It Couldn't Be Done . . .

At the same time he was securing funding, Justin was also setting up his manufacturing process. His new contacts in the industry had explained that most specialty food products are made by contract manufacturers, or co-packers, so one of Justin's first steps would be to find a facility that would make his nut butters. And as he started writing his business plan, he began contacting large peanut butter companies to see if they could make his nut butter. "I would tell them my rough formula, which I thought was so simple—almonds and maple syrup, or peanuts and honey—and they all said they couldn't do that on their equipment," he remembers. "In fact, most said that it couldn't be done anywhere."

The problem was that most nut butter manufacturers use grinders to mash the peanuts, and the honey or maple syrup called for in Justin's recipes would heat up during the grinding process and gunk up their machines. Usually, companies avoid this problem by using sugar because it doesn't stick to the machines (and is cheaper, to boot). A frustrated Justin was on the phone with yet another co-packer when inspiration struck: "This is ridiculous," he told them. "I have no problem doing this at home, and you're supposed to be the expert with all of the fancy equipment? How come I can do it, and you can't?"

And that's when Justin had his aha moment. In his own kitchen, he was using a food processor, not a nut grinder, and somehow, that was making all the difference. So Justin bought an industrial-size food processor and decided to manufacture on his own, eschewing the common route of co-packers. "Looking back, it's one of the best things I did," he says. "Not only was I able to make the exact recipes I wanted but I ended up with a really distinctive flavor and texture that our competitors can't touch. To this day, I still use food processors, and the way I use them has even become a trade secret."

Justin found a salsa company in Denver that had FDA-certified kitchen space, and negotiated to rent it on nights and weekends for a reduced rate. Even though it meant a long drive and working at odd hours, it fit into his low-cost start-up mode. And with his manufacturing process and funding in place, Justin was finally ready to make some nut butters.

The Long Trek

So began the two slow years of building the business from scratch: waiting tables full-time, making peanut butter in every remaining hour he could find, and selling it at the farmers' markets on the weekends.

Justin's ultimate goal was to get his nut butters in the local Whole Foods. In the meantime, he dropped by smaller stores like the Boulder branch of Great Harvest Bread Co., who immediately agreed to stock the jars and became his first account. "But Whole Foods was where I really wanted to be. I figured that once you make it there, you're all set," says Justin. "You can pretty much relax, go on vacation, and have a bestselling food product. As I'm sure everyone except me realized, that's not the case!"

But Justin kept talking to the Whole Foods buyer, whom he'd met purely out of naiveté. "I walked in to the customer service desk and politely asked who their buyer was, and remarkably, he came out to talk to me," remembers Justin. "He either thought my nut butters were a good idea or simply wanted to get rid of me for the moment, because he asked to see some samples."

The next day, Justin was at Whole Foods bright and early with jars of all his flavors. But he didn't just drop them off; he also asked the buyer for constructive criticism. "You know, I think this could use a little more salt and this could use a little more cinnamon, and that could use a little less honey," responded the buyer as he tasted his way through the line. In a stroke of inspiration, Justin took the feedback and tweaked the recipes just a touch, so the buyer felt like he'd co-developed the flavors and felt obligated to bring the nut butters in, just as Justin had suspected. But even with that approval, there were still lots of objections that Justin needed to overcome.

First, Justin would need to use Whole Foods's distributor because the buyer didn't want to order 5,000 items from 5,000 different companies; he wanted to place an order with just one distributor. But Justin's Nut Butters was too small for the grocery behemoth's distributor, which wouldn't work with him until he increased in size. "How about if I deliver the product myself?" he asked the buyer.

The buyer agreed, but how would the jars get to the shelves? It'd be just another item to look out for. "I'll deliver *and* stock the shelves!" countered Justin. "I'll even take inventory and charge you for only what you need to fill the shelf."

"Well, what if it doesn't sell well and I'm out for the cases I ordered?" came the reply. Justin was ready: "I'll give you your first case for free; if it doesn't sell, you can give it away and not incur a single penny of loss." And if it sold slowly—or not at all—Justin would give samples to the staff and customers. To top it all off, if his nut butters weren't selling successfully in three months he'd kick himself out.

Finally, Justin made it through the line of arguments: He was in! The nut butters were set up for sale at that single store, but once they were in the system, it would be easier for any of the twenty Whole

Foods in the Rocky Mountain region to begin carrying them. Justin was ready to use that fact to his advantage.

Soon Justin had his nut butters in fifteen stores. He'd deliver, stock the shelves, and do demos each weekday, then pull a night shift at a restaurant. On the weekends, he'd head to the kitchen and make his blends for twelve hours at a time. And for two years, this was Justin's nonstop schedule.

Slowly, order by order, he started seeing success. When he couldn't produce enough nut butter on the weekends to meet demand, he knew it was time to rent his own, full-time facility. "Ironically, I rented the kitchen from a company that had just declared bankruptcy," remembers Justin. "When I signed the lease, the owners told me that the place was haunted and filled with bad luck." But he needn't have worried; after just a few days in his new digs, he had the idea that would propel Justin's Nut Butters into the national market: squeeze packs.

I Dream of Squeeze Packs

Even though the nut butters were doing well, Justin still needed a "real" job to pay the bills. After years of waiting tables, he transitioned to working at REI, the backpacking and outdoors store. And it was while he was organizing product there, lining up the single serve carbohydrate packs that were all the rage for runners and bikers, that he got his genius idea. "What if we did a protein pack—a single serving of a real food, sized for athletes and made for on-the-go consumption?" he wondered. His company already made great peanut and almond butters, but they were packaged in full-size jars, like every other nut butter out there. Would little packets set them apart?

By the end of his shift, Justin was taken with the concept. He began calling up every manufacturer he could find who made squeeze packets (like those used for fast-food ketchup—Heinz sells eleven billion of those packs a year). They all had the same response: "There's no way we'll do peanut butter squeeze packets, because peanuts are an allergen and will contaminate our equipment." But Justin couldn't stop thinking about his idea and became convinced that squeeze packets would truly differentiate his nut butters.

In a moment of déjà vu, Justin decided that if he couldn't get his nut butter squeeze packets made, he'd manufacture them himself. But the machines used to make squeeze packets were expensive, so Justin first rewrote his business plan and raised an additional $60,000 to finance his own machine. Of that, $40,000 went toward a used machine—one that was older than Justin and had been used to package hair-conditioner samples back in the 1980s! Then he spent $20,000 to recondition it and format it to make single-serving squeeze packs. Finally, almost a year after he had his brainstorm, Justin lined up his packets in a thirty-count display box and sent it in to REI for consideration.

Although Justin thought REI was the ideal spot for his packets, he also dropped off a box with each of his Whole Foods accounts. They loved the idea, so Justin stocked the squeeze packs with the energy bars, right next to the gels and Clif Bars. "I was ready to roll," remembers Justin. Then REI sent him a form letter, declining to carry the new product. That piece of bad news was immediately followed by a call from the Whole Foods buyer: "Hey, these things really aren't selling. I'm going to take them off the shelf." Had Justin just sent $60,000 straight down the drain?

Instead of getting upset and discouraged, Justin sat down and tried to figure out what was happening. He still thought squeeze packets themselves were a great idea, but something in the placement or marketing wasn't working. He called the buyer at Whole Foods and asked for one favor, drawing on the two years of goodwill he'd built up: "Could I move the squeeze packs next to the peanut butter? I'm going to lose the 'energy pack' label and emphasize the peanut butter." He got his chance. Justin redesigned the label, set the price at 99 cents, and slipped the packets right alongside his regular nut butters. And to his immense relief, they immediately took off. Justin was elated. "In a matter of weeks, I went from despair—I had wasted my life savings, my mother was so ashamed that her son was the founder of a failing peanut butter company—to realizing I could actually do this thing!" he exclaims.

He figured out what had changed: No one knew what the energy packs *were*. Justin's Nut Butters didn't have the branding or marketing money to sell the world on a new food invention, but it could sell the world on good old peanut butter in cute little packets. Next to a full-size jar, the packets became whatever a consumer wanted them to be: travel size, portion-control size, kid size, or, most important, sample size. "Let's say you see something new in the store, like a $10 jar of almond butter," says Justin. "That's pretty expensive. What if you don't like it? It's a risk. But if there's a squeeze packet version of that same almond butter right there, for a dollar, you'll grab that. If you don't like it, well, it's just a dollar. And if you *do* like it, maybe you'll buy the full size next time." Without even meaning to, the squeeze packs became a de facto trial size for Justin's jars, and sales of both finally started soaring, in tandem.

The Power of Equity

The squeeze packs were Justin's ticket to the big time. Whole Foods said they'd take them nationwide. Starbucks wanted to pair them with crackers in a snack box. (Justin had called them virtually a hundred times, and when they finally needed a peanut butter product he was the guy at the top of their minds.) "And then, guess what?" says Justin, laughing. "REI calls me, and they've seen my squeeze packs at other stores—could they carry them?"

After years of work, Justin had suddenly reached the point where he had a successful product (and $1 million in sales to prove it!). While Justin had the product part down pat, his advisers cautioned that investors don't invest in great products: They invest in really talented teams that have experience growing and selling great products. It was time to stop being a one-man show and build a team. First up: Lance Gentry, who had previously been the very first hire at Izze Beverage Company. He had led Izze from a $1 million business to a $25 million business, then orchestrated a sale to Pepsi. Justin knew he'd found his dream president.

The only catch was that Justin's Nut Butters didn't have nearly enough money to hire someone with Lance's expertise, reputation, and experience. Lance put it out there honestly: "Look, I can't work for nothing. I need to bring home money to support my wife and two kids." "What's the minimum you need to cover your expenses for the next few months?" asked Justin. "I'll pay you what you need now in cash, and we can set up the rest of your salary as equity in the company." So for his first year, Lance received an under-market salary plus equity for his compensation package, then eventually converted to a full-cash salary. "Equity compensation was the only way I could afford someone at that level, and I'm so glad I did it," explains Justin. He then took that idea of equity as compensation and used it again multiple times throughout the growth process, for everything from investors and employees to designers and brokerage firms.

But back in 2008, it was still just Justin and Lance, and together they now had credibility with the investment community. Even as the economy collapsed, they raised the $1.2 million they needed to execute their revised business plan. They decided to work with *angel investors*, people and firms who invest anywhere from $100,000 to $1 million in a company during the start-up or growth phase. In the end, they signed deals with sixty different angel investors (most from the Colorado area) to reach their monetary goal—and to ensure that no single investor would have a large, controlling stake in Justin's Nut Butters.

Creating a Clean Design

Justin's packaging was originally a colorful, vibrant, Ben & Jerry's–type kaleidoscope. It was perfect when they were a local, bootstrapping brand, but as the company grew, the design needed to appeal to a broader audience. That meant a logo and packaging that was clean and timeless. Justin's was selling a premium, white tablecloth nut butter, but consumers couldn't tell that from the package.

Justin and Lance went to the advertising company that had worked with Izze, TDA Advertising and Design, and commissioned them to redesign the Justin's logo and label. And of course, Justin's Nut Butters was still a small company and didn't have the type of money it would normally cost to design a product line, especially with a high-end advertising firm like TDA.

So again Justin turned to his one valuable asset: equity. Together, they worked out a blended deal—a little bit of ownership, a little bit of cash. Although not everyone is open to equity in lieu of a paycheck (because it's technically worthless until the company is sold, has dividends, or pays you back), it was the perfect compromise in this case. TDA came up with Justin's new packaging: a simple cartoon-esque nut against a sparkling white background, with *Justin's* written in handwriting-like cursive. It was just the thing for Justin's national roll out.

Building a Team

For Justin, smart use of his equity also ended up being the ticket to attracting the best talent at a price he could afford. Today, all of Justin's employees are equity owners: "Everyone who works for us is paid a below-market salary, and they're working twice as hard because that's how I work. I'm underpaid and I'm working twice as hard. But I own the company," says Justin. "It makes sense that I'd work hard. So every employee owns a small piece of the company as well." The exact amounts vary—executives receive more equity than entry-level workers—but Justin says that as a result, everyone treats the business like it's his or her own: "We're very mindful with how we spend money or about staying late or coming in early to finish a project. It's definitely a successful strategy." A new employee starting in 2012 would receive a small percentage of an ownership stake, which would vest over four years. (It's part of the company's benefits package, which also includes fun perks like a fridge full of free food and a sports and wellness stipend as well as more standard benefits like health insurance.)

Justin also wanted to create a formal advisory board, made up of people in the community who could act as advisers and provide a level of professionalism that he didn't yet have. He had started with three professors at Colorado University's business school, mentors with whom he'd developed relationships. He eventually transitioned his board to three executives with experience in the natural product sector: John Maggio, the founder of Boulder Canyon Chips; Peter Burns, the CEO of Celestial Seasonings (who stepped down in 2012 due to a conflict of interest and was replaced by Jane Miller of Rudi's Organic Bakery); and Hass Hassan, who had founded and sold a chain of natural grocery stores.

Justin's goal was to surround himself with advisers who had one foot firmly planted in his company's present and the other foot where he wanted to go. John gives him confidence and keeps him grounded; Peter and Jane know how to run a $100 million company; and Hass (who was and is also a board member of Whole Foods) sets them up for success in the future. The advisory board also provides a sense of security for local investors because they know the members. Board membership is generally a paid position, and at the time, of course, Justin had no cash—just equity. He gave each member ownership shares, so everyone had an incentive to truly make the company better: If Justin's Nut Butters did well, they would be financially rewarded.

The next time Justin brought equity into the conversation, he was negotiating a brokerage deal. Food companies often work with a brokerage firm, which acts as a national sales team on behalf of a client. Brokerages have people all over the country who represent a brand to grocery stores and buyers—so company owners don't have to sell, stock, and keep up with, say, every grocery store chain in South Carolina. With a brokerage, Justin and his small staff wouldn't have to jet across the country, trying to land and keep accounts.

Each broker represents thirty to forty different companies and will pitch each product to local grocery store buyers. "But of course, these guys are also really expensive and I couldn't afford them on a monthly

FIVE MISTAKES EVERYONE MAKES IN A BUSINESS PLAN

Mayra Ceja, who runs a start-up consulting firm and a food incubator in Brooklyn, New York, shares the top errors she sees clients making.

1. Writing a business plan for the wrong audience. There are two distinct audiences to consider, and each requires a different mindset. The first audience is you! Write a plan solely as a private exercise, to clarify your idea and business model and think through questions in an orderly fashion. But just because the end results are orderly doesn't mean you have to write in a linear fashion; releasing yourself from that A-B-C mentality can help immensely.

The second business plan is the one you use to raise money. This time, it's about persuading potential investors *why*, exactly, your idea will succeed. Consider using a "SWOT Analysis"—strengths, weaknesses, opportunities, and threats—as a framework for this more official version.

2. Using highfalutin language and concepts. Forget the elaborate templates and instead consider four simple questions: (1) What is my product? (2) What am I charging for it? Consider that most physical products are marked up by a factor of four: The cost is doubled once when you sell to a retailer and again when the retailer sells to a customer. (3) Who am I selling it to?

The answers to the first three questions will go a long way toward answering the fourth, the break-even analysis, that is, (4) Can this business make money?

Maybe the business can make money, but not enough to support your lifestyle. How long are you willing to run it on the side or while funding it from savings or loans? What level of costs and sales would you need for the business to be self-supporting? Would you have to sell 10,000 cookies a year, or 10 million cookies? Not every venture has to be a big, mass-market brand, but it should eventually be sustainable.

3. Not thinking about the medium term. Sure, you want to sell to your local grocery store this month and be a multimillion-dollar business in ten years. But your business plan should look out about two years in the future. Where do you want to be then? A goal to be in Walmart or Whole Foods is a drastically different scenario from selling items at your local corner market. Pick your two-year target, then work backward from those aspirations to see how you could get there.

4. Being afraid of the competition. One of the blind spots I see constantly is when aspiring entrepreneurs neglect to fully research the market. Some don't even use Google to see if their product already exists! They fear that if they *know* about a similar product, they can't create a new version. But competition is really validation that there's a market. Define your space in it: What can you do to differentiate yourself? Do consumers want a product with healthier ingredients or better packaging? Lower prices or a unique background?

And if you *can't* find something similar, why doesn't it exist? There's a reason, and the answer could be good or bad. Maybe you've figured out a business model that finally makes it profitable to produce this product. Maybe consumers weren't previously ready for this product and now they are. But maybe there's no market for your product—others have tried and failed—and you should know that.

The best entrepreneurs I've worked with truly study their competitors and learn from their best practices. Think of it this way:

Your competitor is doing at least something right because they are already succeeding in the market.

5. Not turning your plan into a snazzy pitch deck. After all the work that goes into a business plan, entrepreneurs obviously want someone to read it! But many investors now prefer pitch decks, which are PowerPoint or Prezi presentations that summarize a business idea and succinctly sell it. It's a highlight reel of top points in an exciting, visually compelling, and engaging format. Once investors are intrigued and want to know more, they'll turn to the business plan.

retainer or salary," says Justin. So instead, he turned to his trusty equity play: "We have a hot little brand here with a really strong management team, and someday we'll be able to afford a full payment," he told the owner of the firm. "But what if, until that day, I give you a share of ownership instead?" It worked, and now those brokers are also financially invested in helping Justin's Nut Butters succeed.

What Does Equity Really Mean?

"Leveraging equity was very necessary—I couldn't have grown as quickly or as efficiently without doing it," says Justin. "But you have to remember that at the end of the day, it's not magical free money." Instead, he's giving up ownership and has to constantly make sure he can maintain the 51 percent necessary to remain in full control.

And does all of this emphasis on equity mean Justin's plan is to sell the company someday? Not necessarily, but he had to make it a possibility if he ever wanted substantial investment. "I went everywhere looking for money," explains Justin. That included everything from business plan competitions, to conferences where one entrepreneur after the next pitched ideas, to casual coffees in investors' dining rooms. But everywhere he went, one thing remained the same: the need to offer *x* return on an investment within four to five years.

That return can come in a number of ways, but the most straightforward is with a full acquisition: A brand is bought by a larger brand for cash, and everyone gets paid out all at once. So Justin wrote this clean and simple exit strategy into his business plan. "But the reality is, as long as I'm the majority shareholder, I don't ever have to sell my company," he explains. The only legal and ethical responsibility he has is to pay his investors back, and there are lots of options as to how. For example, Justin could bring on a new investor to pay off the original investors or offer a profitable business as collateral to get a bank loan to use for repayment.

These days, Justin has no plans to sell his nut butter company. "I have a really strong management team. We're having fun, creating innovative product lines, and being challenged," he says. "But if we ever come to a point where we're in over our heads, or we're no longer having fun, or we're no longer creating relevant products, then that's when I would look to exit and pay out a return to all of my investors."

Over the last few years, Justin has seen how rare it is for a founder to grow a company to significant size and still be in complete control (let alone be in business at all!). Instead, many brands that seem independent are actually owned by banking groups. The groups buy a majority stake—usually because the company needs money quickly during a high-growth stage—and then the founder becomes an employee of the banking group. After five or six years, the group sells the brand to a conglomerate like Kellogg's or General Mills. "There's nothing wrong with any of this, but it means the founder has absolutely no control over his or her baby, and that can be very upsetting," says Justin. "So I play the equity card, but one of my top priorities is making sure I maintain control."

Nut Butters . . . and Beyond!

Now back to our story, and the moment when retailers were just starting to clamor for the new squeeze packs. Justin quickly realized that the packs did not sell well on their own; without the jars, they lost their trial-size, mini-me appeal. So he made the dual placement mandatory: If a store wanted to carry the squeeze packs, they had to carry the corresponding jars, too. And, of course, this meant that both parts of the business grew rapidly. While it was win–win for Justin's Nut Butters, grocery managers also loved it because sales of *all* almond butter, both Justin's and other brands, started rising across the board.

By 2010, Justin was ready to launch another nut butter product: candy. "My favorite childhood treats, without a doubt, were Reese's peanut butter cups. I knew I'd love to eat an organic, all-natural version, and it blew my mind that nobody else was doing it," he says. Like the peanut butter squeeze packs, Justin wasn't able to patent the idea; he hadn't invented peanut butter and he hadn't invented squeeze packs, he just put the two together. In the same way, he hadn't invented organic peanut butter and he hadn't invented chocolate, he was just putting them together. But he still saw an opportunity in the market and thought Justin's could be the company to grab it first.

But finding someone who could manufacture a Reese's-like peanut butter cup was harder than Justin had thought. It turned out that anybody who had ever made something similar had either gone out of business or been bought by Hershey's (which makes Reese's). Finally, through word-of-mouth referrals, he found a small, family-owned company that had an old piece of equipment. The machine hadn't been used in years, but Justin essentially talked the owner out of retirement and they were off!

To Justin, the peanut butter cups weren't simply peanut butter cups; they also represented the future of his brand. If they were well received, Justin's Nut Butters could expand into new categories and be taken seriously, and if they weren't, Justin's would forever be a one-hit wonder nut company. With his fingers crossed, Justin presented the new product to Whole Foods in 2011. Luckily, they loved it and launched the product nationwide, where shoppers snapped it up. "That was a turning point. Now we're a food company with 'better-for-you' products," explains Justin. He went on to reverse engineer America's favorite candy bar—that would be Snickers—and came out with a natural version in 2012. With the success of other product lines, it was also time for Justin to transition his company's name: They dropped the *nut butters* and became, simply, Justin's.

Justin's products are now showcased across the grocery store, and he's seeing the power of increased exposure and cross-pollination: there's the nut butter customer, who buys the candy because they already love Justin's. And then there's the candy customer, who might have walked by the nut butters a hundred times before. Now the logo pops out—"Hey, I know this brand!"—and they're more likely to give it a try.

Justin's Three Keys to Success

Today, Justin makes time to constantly pay it forward and work with new entrepreneurs, giving back in the same way others helped him just a few short years ago. He's found that a food entrepreneur needs three things to be successful: passion, a strong work ethic, and extreme self-discipline. "Passion is number one, and everybody knows that. If you're passionate and have a strong work ethic, odds are you're going to work very hard at making your business idea a reality," explains Justin. "But the glue to all of it is that you have to be extremely self-disciplined.

"It's easy to work all day and all night on something you really love, but there will always be parts of the business that you're not as passionate about or as good at. That's where the self-discipline kicks in. It forces you to do the things most entrepreneurs would give up on and separates a successful entrepreneur from a failed one."

Justin pulls out all of his powers of self-discipline when it comes to anything financial. For example, he had to learn how to analyze profit and loss statements: where the money is coming from, how reliable it is, and how they're spending it. "It's been hard for me," he admits freely. "It's not always easy or enjoyable. But I'm living proof that you can do it."

It is, of course, the creative, romantic, and glamorous parts of business that entrepreneurs get excited about: making a product, getting it onto the shelf, dreaming up marketing initiatives, and talking to excited customers. "But behind all of that, your business has to actually make money and be able to sustain its growth," he reminds us. "Or you don't have a business, you have a really expensive hobby."

In 2012, Justin's manufactured about 1.5 million jars and 30 million squeeze packs of peanut butter, which were sold in over 10,000 locations. When Justin looked it up, the numbers shocked even him: "It's unbelievable to me that we do 30 million packs a year. It actually gives me little goose bumps," he says. "I pinch myself all the time."

And finally, it was time for Justin to say good-bye to the last of his roommates, the very ones who had swiped his nut butters from the kitchen cabinet years earlier. Even as his sales exploded, Justin had kept his living expenses as low as possible and taken home just a small salary or none at all. He and his wife even continued to live with the roommates after the wedding, a true measure of their commitment to pouring every last cent back into the company. But finally, with a baby on the way and a business that is officially thriving, they could admit it: Justin Gold's crazy nut butter dream had turned into a reality.

TAKE AWAY

- **Consider hybrid compensation.** Justin was able to bring on the best-of-the-best management team, design firms, brokerages, and more only by using a combination of equity (a share in his company) and cash to cover salaries and fees. While an early operating budget wouldn't let him afford, say, a $300,000 salary, negotiating a deal that resulted in a $100,000 salary and a 1 percent share of the company might.

- **But maintain control.** Leveraging equity allowed Justin to grow his company quickly and efficiently, but it wasn't free money. He stresses that equity is ownership of your company, and it's a common entrepreneurial misstep to give up too much, too soon. It sounds obvious, but realize that you'll need 51 percent to remain in full control—not just now but down the road as you take on additional investment. Don't blow through your whole equity stash at once.

- **Make employees feel invested in your company's success.** By giving board members and all employees—from entry level to top executives—an equity stake, no matter how small, they're incentivized to work extra hard because they have a vested financial interest in the growth and health of the company. Think of it as part of a benefits package (like healthcare) that also encourages people to use valuable company resources wisely (including his or her own time).

7

How Simple Wins on the Grocery Store Shelf

HINT

Kara Goldin throws out all the sugary sodas and juices in her kitchen and tries to convince her family—and eventually, America—that water can be exciting and delicious.

In Search of Simple

In 1995, a little-known company called AOL asked Kara Goldin to run its new concept—an online shopping channel. The gregarious, twenty-eight-year-old redhead gave it a whirl and was soon leading a groundbreaking, flourishing unit. Kara credits its success to the rising wave of online shopping, paired with simplicity. "Consumers like simple," she explains. "They gravitate toward things that are simple to use, simple to understand, and simple to execute. And that's what we did at AOL."

But by 2001, with a toddler and new baby at home and another on the way, Kara's own life was far from simple. She lived in San Francisco, but AOL's offices were in Virginia. For years, her commute started with a 7 a.m. cross-country flight! Both she and her husband, Theo, an attorney, were spending half their lives in planes and cars, grabbing food and sleep wherever they could. During those hectic, jam-packed years, Kara kept returning to her professional motto: "Keep it simple." It was time to implement the same adage in her personal life and leave AOL.

At home with her two (and eventually four) children, Kara began to apply her consumer savvy to simplifying her family's experiences. Now, instead of cutting through all of the white noise of the online shopping world, she was trying to cut through the white noise of family life. She laid a discerning eye on everything from *Sesame Street* to strollers to afternoon snacks. Food was the worst culprit. During her harried AOL days, Kara and her nanny would stock the cupboards with convenience meals and snacks, anything that could be prepared and eaten quickly. Now, with more time to spare, Kara pulled out boxes and started reading the long lists of ingredients, which were far from simple. "I found that almost everything I was eating and drinking was filled with chemicals," says Kara. "Worse, I was giving the same stuff to my children."

Kara quietly started brainstorming ways her family could change the way they ate. She needed a challenge that was significant but doable. What about the five-cups-a-day juice habit her kids had developed? While a little juice could be healthy, that amount of concentrated, sugar-laden beverage most definitely was not. She broached the idea to her husband: What if they made water, simple water, their default drink? Theo looked at her, incredulous: "What about *your* Diet Coke habit?" He had a point: Kara had been a loyal soda fan for more than twenty years, relying on the caffeine for much needed kicks during late work nights and jet-lag fogs.

If her kids were going to go cold turkey on juice, Kara would do

Courtesy Hint

Kara and Theo Goldin and their children

the same with Diet Coke. She cleaned out the kitchen and put everyone on good old tap water—a moratorium that lasted all of two weeks. "I found that instead of drinking juice and soda, everybody, including me, was drinking . . . nothing," she says. "After a cup or two a day, water was boring us to tears. So instead, we weren't drinking at all."

Kara knew she had to change something or she'd have a home full of dangerously dehydrated kids. Her eyes drifted around the kitchen, looking for an idea, and landed on the big bowl of fruit on her counter, part of her new attempt to stock the house with real, wholesome foods. Kara chopped up a handful, tossed it in a pitcher, added water, and put it in the fridge to chill. A few hours later, she poured a glass to try. It was interesting. It had taste. It was . . . delicious. She poured another glass, and then some for Theo and her kids. Everyone approved! Kara had stumbled on the trick that would make water appealing to her family.

Thrilled, Kara started concocting all sorts of variations, and Theo and her kids were brimming with ideas for new flavors. For example, Kara would crack open a pomegranate and stick it in a pitcher of water, rind, seeds, and all. The process took a total of about twenty seconds. There was no juicing, peeling, or fine dicing involved, just big pieces of fruit that infused the water with flavor. The inedible parts would be left behind when the drink was strained out. Soon, there was always a pitcher brewing in the fridge. And when the kids and their friends stampeded through the house they'd happily grab Kara's fruit water.

Then one day Kara got a phone call from a mother down the street. "My daughter said she had some raspberry water at your house, and she loved it. Where did you get it? What's in it?" "It's just raspberries and water," replied Kara. "But how much sugar did you add?" came the reply. "My daughter is addicted to juice and I always try to water down her apple juice, but she doesn't like it."

Kara, who had added not so much as a sprinkle of sugar to the water, had an epiphany: "I was starting with plain water and adding fruit to give it flavor. But when you start with a drink like apple juice and water it down or change the ingredients to make it lighter or less sugary, you're changing a product that used to be enjoyable. Then it feels like you're compromising." And the lower-sugar and lower-calorie products available in supermarkets were also compromises: they took the sugar out and replaced it with synthetic sweeteners, which never tasted as good as the original. But what if Kara had a beverage that wasn't, at heart, a compromise—but an upgrade?

Kara tucked the upgrade idea in the back of her mind. A few weeks later, she was at the gym when a friend spied the water-pomegranate mix Kara had brought along for a workout, took a sip, and couldn't stop raving. The resounding hymn of Kara's career rang out in her head: What does the consumer need? They didn't need sugar waters filled with all sorts of unpronounceable ingredients. They needed the simple product, and Kara had just had her second epiphany.

Have Water, Will Sell

Kara raced home to tell Theo about what had happened at the gym, and about the little girl who loved the raspberry water. "We should make this and sell it!" she exclaimed. When Theo gently reminded her that she was a technology executive, one who didn't know the first thing about the beverage industry or manufacturing, Kara was undeterred. She'd figure it out.

Kara headed to the most obvious place for information she could think of: her local Whole Foods, where she walked up to the first official-looking person she saw. "I've got this great idea for a product, and I want to know how I get it on your shelves," she enthused, rapid-fire style. The stock boy looked up at her and calmly replied: "Well, you'll definitely need to get a UPC code, so that we can scan it with our cash registers." Over the next few weeks, Kara continued to ask question after question. She learned she'd need to find a bottle supplier and caps (and that everyone in the industry called caps *closures*), as well as a certified facility to make the water. Every day, she added to her growing arsenal of knowledge about the beverage industry. First up on her to-do list to conquer: a name.

Kara wanted her flavored waters to be for adults *and* kids, so her original name idea was kid-friendly: wawa. "When we talked about it at home, we had been calling it 'wawa,' like a small child might pronounce *water*," explains Kara. "The thought was that people didn't need or want all these extra ingredients, they just needed good old wawa." That name was quickly killed when they realized there was a chain of convenience stores on the East Coast called Wawa.

So Kara, Theo, and their friends started brainstorming. As Kara described the waters, she kept saying: "It just has a hint of this, or a hint of that." Somebody mused, "What about 'Hint'?" Eyes lit up—*Hint* was *good*. Theo knew their chances of getting a four-letter word trademarked were next to impossible, but they decided to try. They were amazed when the trademark attorney came back with an all clear. "So what exactly is this product? What are you trying to do?" asked the attorney. "We're encouraging people to drink water, not sugar," replied Kara, without giving her answer too much thought. It was the lawyer who instantly saw the tagline potential of her answer: Drink water, not sugar. Hint was officially born; now it was time to actually make the product.

Diving In

Kara found her bottler through good new-fashioned Googling. She didn't know that bottlers—and all food and beverage manufacturers that make products for other companies—are referred to as co-packers, so that was the first hurdle to overcome. Once she deciphered the lingo, Kara began searching for co-packers who would do a small batch of a beverage.

Kara started chatting on the phone with a woman who owned a bottling plant in Chicago, and the two hit it off. "Come on out," the co-packer suggested, "And have a look at what we could do." In the whirl of the new business, Kara had one more new thing brewing:

she was five months pregnant with her fourth child. With that in mind, she asked Theo if he'd come along on the trip for support. So when Kara and Theo walked onto the co-packer floor, they were wowed together. "It was exhilarating," remembers Kara. "We knew how to do our 'real' jobs well and had become reasonably comfortable. And then all of a sudden we were learning so much and a whole world opened up." Kara was already hooked, and now Theo was as well. He thought he'd take a few months off from his legal career and help get Hint up and running—and ended up never going back. He became Hint's chief operating officer, while Kara took on the role of chief executive officer. Together, they signed up for a production run, took $50,000 out of their bank account to use as a start-up fund, and began to make Hint.

Bridge over Troubled Waters

Soon, however, they ran into the straw that would almost break Hint's back: shelf life. They were using a technique called cold-fill, which meant they didn't heat the water or fruits to a boiling point. The process was very similar to what Kara had been making at home for years, but it brought its own safety issues: boiling is one of the surest ways to kill off all sorts of long-living germs. Flavor experts kept telling Kara and Theo that cold-fill was the only option because heating the fruits and vegetables would fundamentally change the taste. "Compare the flavor of a raw carrot versus a cooked carrot—it's very, very different," explains Kara. "In the same way, a fresh strawberry tastes nothing like the warmed strawberries on top of pancakes or oatmeal. I wanted to make sure our product really tasted like a raw carrot or a raw strawberry, so of course I didn't want to heat it."

Unfortunately, she and Theo also wanted to create a product that had no sweeteners, no preservatives, and few or no calories. With a cold-fill, no-preservative product, the longest shelf life anyone could come up with was three months. "Three months?" says Kara. "When I first launched the product, that seemed great. What was everyone worried about?" But she soon realized that she wouldn't always be able to drive down to Whole Foods in her Jeep Cherokee and drop off a batch of freshly brewed Hint waters. While the local store let her sell directly in the beginning, they were upfront and said that if this took off, Hint would need to go through the standard distributor protocol. The distribution chain meant that cases of Hint would first go to a national center, and then weeks—or months—later, they would be shipped out to various supermarkets. And for that, Kara would need at least a six-month shelf life or she'd end up with a lot of expired product being pulled off shelves.

Kara and Theo looked at numerous co-packing options in their quest to extend Hint's shelf life. The closest match she found was a technique called aseptic, which was widely used in Europe but hadn't achieved commercial success in the United States. To their dismay, it was also too expensive for the price point Hint wanted to hit; it had been used exclusively for premium milk products, which could command a higher price. The biggest clincher, though, was that it would keep the water fresh just until the six-month mark, and Kara and Theo were realizing that if the minimum requirement was six months, in reality they'd need their product to last even longer.

After months of persistent searching, they were out of new leads. "I reached a point where I just wanted the idea to go somewhere, and I really didn't know how to manufacture the product with a viable shelf life," Kara says. "I began to believe that we *couldn't* do it, but maybe a large, established company—with millions of dollars of resources and substantial know-how—could."

A friend of a friend at a large international beverage company introduced Kara to someone at a high level of the company whom she could call. Kara rang him up and explained that she was selling these flavored waters at the Whole Foods in San Francisco, and they were doing well, but she'd run into problems with the shelf life. Would they be interested in taking over the product? "I didn't feel like I had enough distribution to even put a dollar figure on the company, but I was essentially ready to throw in the towel if he would launch the product," remembers Kara.

The executive was straightforward with Kara. "We've been in this business a long time," he said. "And we know what customers want: more and more sweetness with fewer and fewer calories. Your flavored water doesn't sound sweet enough. It might sell in a few places like San Francisco, but it'll never take off nationally."

The unequivocal brush-off was just the push Kara needed to come back with a vengeance and prove that the manager was wrong about American consumers. They *did* want something like Hint, Kara believed, and they weren't going to unthinkingly put up with sugar-laden, chemical-filled beverages forever. Kara looked at the black-and-white facts again: She was either going to have to add preservatives or heat the product. There was no third option. Kara was adamant about no preservatives, so she chose heat. She'd just have to ignore the expert opinions and find a way to solve the flavor conundrum.

Kara and Theo had known all along that they couldn't merely throw a pomegranate or piece of pineapple into a water bottle and call it Hint; they'd need a clean, streamlined, and most important, shelf-stable way to get that slight whisper of fruit into pure water. In her early kitchen experiments, Kara gently condensed fruits and vegetables down until she was left with just the oils and skins. She then turned these into low-calorie "essences" that evoked the specific flavor and smell components that define a fruit or vegetable. Now Theo found that by tweaking the flavors throughout the process they were able to compensate for the addition of heat. For example, he could achieve that archetypal blackberry taste by combining blackberries with other fruit or vegetable ingredients to enhance the original flavor. The unstoppable team had solved the riddle; they had true-to-life flavors that were also safe and long lasting. In April 2007, Hint converted to hot-fill production and finally achieved that elusive, nine-month shelf life. (And by 2008, they worked their way up to an eighteen-month shelf life.)

The Truth About Money

After they figured out shelf life, pieces started to fall into place for Hint. They went to one of the NASFT Fancy Food trade shows and received lots of interest from store buyers and press. Then Whole Foods introduced Kara to the giant distributor of the natural food world, UNFI, and she thought she was on easy street. If UNFI thinks that Whole Foods is keen on a product, they're likely to pick it up. "UNFI wants to have a sense that you'll flourish on a national level," explains Kara. "And they want to ensure that you have enough money to keep your business running because it's expensive. It's much more expensive than I had ever anticipated."

The $50,000 Kara and Theo had started with was long gone, and they continued to pour more of their own savings into the company. As they started to see success, friends and family approached and asked if they could invest in the venture. While more money was ostensibly a good thing, Kara and Theo were incredibly cautious about saying yes. "We felt we didn't deserve to take anyone else's money until we proved ourselves," says Kara. "I'm a big believer that you should fund the initial stages yourself or not do it at all. That seed money should be from your hard work and in your name, whether it's a loan from friends or family, savings, or credit card advances. Don't try to raise outside capital before you have a track record."

Today, a lot of aspiring entrepreneurs come to Kara and Theo for advice. Before they have a single product on the shelf they ask: "Who are your investors? Can I talk to them?" "There's no way you're going to get worthwhile investors when your product is still an idea," says Kara. "You have to prove that it can actually sell on the shelf, especially in today's economy." Entrepreneur reality TV shows like *Shark Tank* demonstrate what Kara believes is the worst approach—early-stage companies trading 50 percent or more of their equity for a relatively small amount of investment dollars. After the start-up phase, a company requires significantly more capital to grow, and if you've already traded away a large percentage of equity you're going to be in trouble. "You're certainly not going to be able to control the business decisions," says Kara. "And where's the fun in that? That's why we were wary and have taken on only one significant investor, well after we'd established ourselves as dominant players in this market space."

Selling from Sea to Shining Sea

Kara and Theo wanted to put Hint to the test: Was this a brand and concept that could truly succeed nationally? Was it worth the personal money they were pouring in? Theo, a born-and-bred New Yorker,

KEEPING IT SIMPLE: RESTAURANT EDITION

Michael Chernow and Daniel Holzman of the Meatball Shop, a popular fast-casual chainlet in New York City, share the lessons they've learned along the way.

1. Let your location inspire the food. In restaurants, as in real estate, the mantra may as well be: location, location, location. "It's one of the most important things and usually more important than the food, the concept, or great marketing," says Michael. "It's very difficult to secure an exact location without financing, and you need a business plan to get financing. But knowing the area you plan to be in—as specific as possible—is important." Michael and Daniel specified that they wanted to be within a two-block radius on the Lower East Side, and then went out to find an actual place.

Their concept was still undecided (Fast food? Fast casual? Fine dining?) when Michael and Daniel found a spot they loved. It happened to have a take-out window, which got them thinking. What could they serve to the hordes of late-night partygoers who walked by on their way to the nearby subway stop? Michael thought back to a home-style Italian joint he'd once worked at. "My favorite dish was the rigatoni ragù, a big bowl of pasta with meatballs," he says. "But to keep it lighter and healthier, I'd order it without the rigatoni and add broccoli and spinach. That was my dinner three or four nights a week." Was any restaurant out there all about simple, good old *meatballs*? "So that's what we thought we'd do, solely out of the take-out window: paper bowls filled with meatballs and a stick of focaccia bread for $5. We'd sell it only after midnight, and it would be an underground, unadvertised secret," says Daniel. "Our real restaurant would be something more . . . upscale and practical."

But when the location fell through, Michael and Daniel looked at each other. What if they still tried the meatball idea they'd grown attached to as the real concept for their restaurant? It was decided. Hello, Meatball Shop.

2. Make your menu simple. Once Michael and Daniel had their meatball concept, their next step was to come up with a menu. They wanted meatballs (beef, pork, veggie), a rotating daily special, and sides of greens, roasted vegetables, bread, polenta, and risotto. "The most important thing, whenever you have disparate elements on a menu, is to have some sort of theme that runs through everything," says Daniel. "You don't want to eat a bite of curried cauliflower after you've had a bite of sweet-and-sour pork. Because our menus are mix and match, we have to be especially careful and make sure that our dishes go together in any combination. So some are more neutral (like cheesy polenta) and some have more assertive flavors."

But the main fact that keeps all of those menu items working together is simplicity. "Simple is best," says Michael. "The more complicated the menu and the flavors are, the more complicated everything else gets. We have a pretty simple concept to begin with, and we're constantly working to keep things simple."

3. Remember that food costs are only one part of the big picture. It can cost anywhere from $350,000 to $900,000 just to get a restaurant to opening day. "It depends on so many factors, like your concept and geographic area. More money gives you more choices," says Daniel. "Of course, if you have no money, you can find a hole in the wall that's basically a garbage dump, install a stove, and call it a restaurant for $20,000."

Then there are the basic operating margins that you need to hit to keep a restaurant afloat. Michael explains: "Start with your total gross sales, which equals 100 percent. Food is only a small piece of the puzzle: You want to keep food costs below 30 percent, labor costs below 35 percent, and rent below 10 percent. Then all of your miscellaneous costs add up (like inspections and permits) to about 13 percent, and you hope you end up with an 8 to 12 percent profit. If you get more than that, you're really excited; if you get a little less than that, you're happy you can just stay afloat. If you get much less than that, you go out of business."

4. The restaurant industry is a twenty-four-hour business. "Whether you have a place that's open from 7 a.m. to 2 p.m., or five in the afternoon until two in the morning, the work isn't done when your restaurant closes," says Michael. "People are constantly trying to get in touch with you." He wishes he had drawn a line in the sand in the very beginning: "This is when I will be available to respond to people, and this is when I won't." Instead, he let it become a 24/7 situation, responding to emails and phone calls all day and night long. "But you need to carve out a period of time, even if it's only an hour, when people know that they will not, and cannot, reach you," he says. "That's the only way to have a restaurant, and some semblance of a personal life."

5. Always plan a best-case scenario. Michael and Daniel remodeled and set up their new restaurant themselves, painting, hammering away, and testing out countless variations of meatballs. When Michael jokes about working in an unheated room all winter long, Daniel reminds him that their place was "the first restaurant opening in the history of New York to come in on time and under budget." But within a few weeks of selling their first meatballs, something completely unplanned and shocking sneaked up on the guys. "We made all of these worst-case scenario and 'if we're just hanging on by a thread' plans," explains Michael. "But luck was on our side, and we ended up being much more successful than we had ever anticipated. We had never made a best-case scenario plan, so we hadn't thought about how to handle a huge overflow of customers or quickly expand our food order or what to say to all of the people who were asking us to open Meatball Shops in their neighborhoods. Not to say it isn't wonderful, but you should always have a plan for what you'll do if everything goes right. Because it might!"

knew exactly what it would take for him to feel confident about the future viability of Hint: A successful New York City launch.

Kara turned to her old friends who lived in the city. Did they have any ideas? A friend who was throwing parties during the Tribeca Film Festival suggested that Kara could put out chilled bottles of her waters at the events. It would be a way to get the products into the hands of influential New Yorkers and could be a first baby step into the market.

Kara thought it was a good plan and went one step further. Wouldn't it be nice if she could tell people where to find Hint in the neighborhood? Kara found a small independent grocery store near the parties called Gourmet Garage. She called up and explained that she was launching an unsweetened, flavored water during the film festival and she'd love to have it available for sale nearby. When the woman on the phone expressed interest, Kara kept going. They'd had success in San Francisco, but Gourmet Garage would be their very first East Coast store.

The woman on the line said, "Great! I'll take ten cases."

"Wow. Really? You're going to take ten cases?" gasped a shocked Kara.

"Yeah," came the reply. "Why don't you send me a couple samples, but this sounds like it would do well in my market."

"Would you mind faxing an order over?" asked Kara, remembering to execute fully on the deal.

"You want me to pay for the cases?" asked the woman, incredulous.

Kara would later find out that many new companies give boxes of product to stores for free, a practice she never adopted. "Yeah, just fax it over," she replied. "And then if you could just give me a credit card number or write a check and send it as soon as you can, that would be really great." Kara didn't know if she'd made a watershed sale, or whether her naive, grassroots approach had scared away Gourmet Garage for life.

But the woman did send the check, sold the Hint waters, and then bought more and sold more. Hint officially had a New York presence, and people were buying their product. "But it's still a joke in our office, even today, because that experience was completely unconventional," says Kara. "It's not the way retailers typically work. They rarely do business over the phone and rarely stock something without having even sampled it." Normally, a sales strategy involves meeting the buyer and forming a personal connection with him or her, and then he or she *might* think about looking at a product. "But out of the blue, this woman decided to take a chance on us," continues Kara. "Today, she's a big buyer for Whole Foods—her name is also Kara—and I love to tell her that her order launched us in New York City!"

With that, Kara and Theo were confident their product had staying power. They signed up with a direct store delivery (DSD) firm, a distributor that works exclusively with beverages, as well as UNFI. "We thought, 'Wow. This is great. Now we have all these distributors and our product will magically be everywhere,'" says Kara.

Not so fast. They soon learned that distributors are delivery vehicles. That's it; their only formal job is to get the product to the store on time and in perfect condition. Kara and her growing team of employees would have to sell buyers on the product themselves. Today, Kara has a team of thirty sales employees and growing: "That's what it takes to get into lots and lots of stores," she says. "It's all about the sales *you* make."

Hint's goal was not just to get on the grocery store shelves, but to get lots of exposure and recognition on those shelves. Kara and Theo quickly figured out that the number of SKUs (different flavors) available made an exponential difference in sales: Four SKUs lined up next to each other made a visual impression that caught the consumer's attention, while two SKUs blended in like beverage camouflage.

Once the Hint team realized this, it was just a matter of thinking like a grocery store buyer. "Look at the situation from their point of view," advises Kara. "They're naturally inclined to put beverages on the shelf that they believe will sell and return a profit. Otherwise, they'll eventually lose their job." So Kara's team makes it easy for a buyer to see increased exposure for Hint as a win–win situation. They go into sales meetings armed with lots of real data: how Hint stacks up to the beverages already on that particular store's shelves, comparisons in sales when a store carries four SKUs versus two SKUs, and which varieties sell best in that region.

The second part of their sales pitch is explaining why the shoppers who stroll down grocery and convenience store aisles nationwide *want* Hint. "Sure, if everybody liked to drink plain tap water, then I'd be out of a job," says Kara. "But the fact is, they don't. There will always be those people who aren't satisfied with water, and Hint solves that problem. That's how we approach retailers—with a problem we've solved."

Once they're in a store, the Hint team doesn't sit down and congratulate themselves; their next goal is always to get *more* exposure and *more* shelf space. "There are places where we have five feet of space on the shelf, because we've proven to the buyers that consumers want

Hint and that sales rise exponentially as our bottles become easier to see and find," says Kara. Again, she focused on her credo of simplicity: What did the customer, in this case, the grocery store buyer, want? They want to sell more product. So Hint's winning strategy focuses on how, exactly, Hint helps the buyer do that.

Making Hint into a Powerhouse Product

Kara also took a deep dive into her growing wealth of sales data to refine the Hint flavors: What should her collection of biggest hits include? Originally, she had designated two flavors—apple and tropical fruit—as Hint Kids. The first two varieties she and Theo had assumed would be more adult-friendly—cucumber and tangerine—were labeled as Hint. "But we found that adults really liked the apple and tropical fruit but felt silly walking around with a bottle that said 'Hint Kids,'" says Kara. Would marketing one product line be simpler than two? That's all Kara had to ask herself; the answer was yes. She and Theo decided to combine everything under a single Hint name and let consumers decide for themselves whether it was a beverage for a kid or an adult.

The popularity of the kids' flavors with adults led Kara to a larger realization: The exotic flavor combinations she'd created, geared toward adventurous foodies, weren't selling nearly as well as the more basic varieties. Blends like cucumber and honeydew hibiscus and hibiscus vanilla were polarizing. They weren't mainstream enough for people to easily understand. But there had to be some flavors that everyone liked: What were they?

Kara looked at the bestsellers in the produce section: strawberries, raspberries, kiwi, mango, watermelon. If those were the flavors that the average consumer already liked, then those were the flavors that could best provide a transition to unsweetened water. So Kara went back to the waters she kept in her refrigerator: uncomplicated combinations, using only what she could pull out of the countertop fruit bowl.

Hint still sells some more unconventional flavors—cucumber water and pear water, for example—but without the same expectations. And the sales team encourages grocery buyers to stock the top five or six bestselling SKUs, instead of picking their more unusual ones. As Kara's keep-it-simple strategy suggests, she wants to give the buyer the products she knows will move off the shelves. "Now there are flavored water brands that highlight their use of herbs, or spices," she says. "That's not Hint. Hint has a mainstream profile and is really about helping your everyday consumer drink water that tastes better."

Smooth Waters

Five years after Kara and Theo sold their first bottle of Hint, the fruit-flavored water was making guest appearances on primetime TV shows like *Grey's Anatomy* and *CSI* and was the beverage of choice at Silicon Valley tech campuses. (Google employees drank so much they even referred to it as their official beverage!) Kara couldn't walk into a grocery store in Alabama or a Starbucks in Maine without seeing Hint on display. She and Theo launched a second line, carbonated Hint Fizz, and even began to look outside the beverage category into other healthy products.

What does Kara wish she'd known a decade ago, when she first tossed her beloved Diet Cokes in the garbage? "Running this business takes a village," she says. "It takes untold money and resources to build it out." For example, even though Hint was sold in 20,000 stores and grew 90 percent in 2012, they're still not at a technical break-even point. Kara explains that Hint could break even in a heartbeat if that was their growth strategy, but for now, she and Theo believe that it's more important to hire employees and continue to expand their reach, a common approach for high-growth businesses.

Today, Kara is thrilled to help shape the zeitgeist of the moment: People are becoming conscious of the effects of sugars, chemicals, and preservatives and want to make changes. And because Hint is on the shelves in over *half* the grocery stores across the country, her influence is substantial. "We're providing a simple, straightforward solution to that customer desire," she says. "Drink water, not sugar. So simple, and so life changing."

TAKE AWAY

- **Your product should solve a common problem.** In Kara's case, it was boredom with tap water. It turned out that lots of other people experience the same issue. Hint solves that problem with a no-sugar, flavored take on regular water, and the problem-solution story is what they bring to retailers.

- **Know when to compromise.** After Kara exhausted all her shelf-life options, she finally realized she would either have to add preservatives or heat the product. Kara was adamant about no preservatives, so she chose heat. But if she'd continued to hold on to both factors as nonnegotiables, Hint would never have made it to the national market.

- **Keep flavors and options simple.** Whether it's fruit water or types of meatballs, customers want simple and straightforward. Find your biggest hits and promote them double-time instead of creating a larger product line, and remember that everyday crowd pleasers result in more sales than gourmet or exotic items.

- **Think like a grocery buyer.** He or she needs to put products on the shelf that sell, so don't talk about what the buyers can do for *you*—sell them on what you can do for *them*. What strategies can you point to (and back up with actual data) that allow a store to sell more? In Hint's case, a certain amount of shelf space and specific flavors result in an exponential increase in sales, and that's a win-win for everyone.

8

Creating Buzz

POPCHIPS

Keith Belling knew that there had to be a snack that wouldn't make him feel as guilty as his daily potato chips did. Could he create and market a new chip that would win over Americans, "one snacker at a time"?

Spare Me the Guilt Chip

Keith Belling had a lunch routine: He'd drop by the neighborhood deli, pick up a sandwich and a bag of chips, and head to the cash register. But one day in early 2005, Keith noticed that he had been subconsciously slipping his chips under his sandwich while he waited in line to pay, effectively hiding them from view. The exuberant Keith, whose lightly graying hair was the only hint that he was closer to fifty than to forty, had to laugh. Did he not want anyone to see his Doritos habit? Or was he hiding the chips from . . . himself? If he was feeling that way about the chips, realized Keith, then maybe he shouldn't be eating them in the first place. But he *did* like his daily dose of deep-fried, salty chips. There had to be something better in the snack aisle that was both delicious *and* more healthful, right?

Courtesy Popchips

Patrick Turpin (left) and Keith Belling

Keith picked up soy crisps, rice cakes, and baked chips, determined to find a new daily snack. Unconvinced, he'd try more brands and flavors, until he had to admit it: He just did not like the taste. That's when Keith's entrepreneurial gene (he had previously launched and sold businesses like AllBusiness.com) kicked in. If he couldn't find a better way to satisfy his daily chip craving, then maybe he could make one. Keith called up his friend Pat Turpin, who had been part of the AllBusiness.com team and who had also run Costco's snack manufacturing business. Pat, another avid snacker, listened to Keith's idea and had only one question. Could they be partners? In June 2005, the friends sealed their deal with a handshake and went out to see what they could find.

They started researching the snack aisle and various food-manufacturing techniques, hoping to jump-start an idea. Pat had a lead that a rice cake manufacturing business in southern California was for sale, and even though they weren't into rice cakes, maybe something there would inspire them. Keith set up a visit and was taken on a tour; within moments, the symbolic light bulb in his head went off. He realized that rice cakes were made by applying heat and high pressure until rice literally popped, and he saw that you could pop all sorts of other things—including potatoes. "It dawned on me that you could actually *pop* potato chips," says Keith. "It wasn't fried. It wasn't baked. It was just what I'd been looking for." He figured that if the 800-pound gorillas in the industry, aka the big consumer packaged goods (CPG) companies, couldn't create that healthy fried chip or tasty baked one, neither could he. Instead, he'd approach the problem from a different angle and create a third category—a new paradigm. "I needed a fresh way to talk to consumers, without the concepts of fried or baked," says Keith. "And that's where pop came in."

Keith was in luck because the rice cake factory was already making a rudimentary version of the popped potato chip, so he knew it could be done. Unfortunately, their product was, at best, average tasting and would need some love to become delicious. The company was churning out items for private label (generic) brands, and there was no flavor development, branding, or marketing to speak of. But if the process was possible, then Keith and Pat knew they could do it better. Just one big question remained: Would consumers want it? Keith knew how to find out.

Survey Says

Keith loved the idea of a popped potato chip, and his gut told him it would work. But if they were going to buy this rice cake plant then he wanted to go on a little more than instinct. Keith and Pat put the business under contract, and then had a short window of time to conduct due diligence. If anything came up, they could still back out. Keith immediately headed to an online survey website called Zoomerang (zoomerang.com), and took his questions straight to regular customers.

He bought a group of 100 snackers (the company will find consumers who fit into a desired target market; in this case, people who identified themselves as snackers) and designed a short survey with multiple-choice questions and fill-in-the-answer blanks. "What do you think of fried chips?" he asked. The replies were exactly what he'd anticipated: "Great tasting, but not healthy." Next up was, "What do you think of baked chips?" Almost every respondent said something like, "If I eat them, it's by default because they're the only option. They taste like cardboard." Then Keith's survey asked, "What does *popped* mean to you?" He was looking for the first adjectives that came to mind. "The words were great," he says. "Things like *yummy*, *healthy*, and *light*."

Finally, he hit them with the big question: "If there were a way to pop a potato chip, what would you think about that?" Keith purposefully left out any mention of the nutritional profile so he wouldn't lead respondents to certain answers. Of the 100 snackers, 85 said they liked the idea of a popped potato chip and wanted to try it. Keith's eyes lit up; here was an exceptionally good response, which gave him faith that customers would be open to a world of popped chips. In October 2005, Keith and Pat closed the deal on the rice cake plant.

Keith and Pat saw the manufacturing facility as a platform to create a whole new business, but they weren't ready to shut down the existing private label operation quite yet. It was still profitable, and those incoming profits would help offset the costs they were about to incur as they developed and marketed their new product. Their plan was to eventually transition out of the rice cake business as they grew their popped potato chip business. But now it was time for Keith and Pat to divide and conquer. Pat's job was to take over the facility (which happened to be a short drive from his home) and run the financial and manufacturing operations, while Keith headed back to San Francisco to hire a team, create a product, build their brand, and lead the sales and marketing.

Making a New Chip Off the Block

Keith had already had his aha moment, so creating the product line was relatively straightforward. He and Pat also had personal capital and early investment money to launch their venture—not unlimited funds but enough to hire specialized, dedicated firms to help at certain steps along the way. First, Keith hired a local food-development firm, signing up a team of their food technologists and chefs. They understand the science of food, but just as important, they understand what delicious tastes like. When Keith asked for a BBQ flavor, or a sour cream and onion flavor, they knew just what all-natural ingredients to use to create that taste profile. For any given flavor, they'd come up with ten to fifteen varieties, then tweak the ingredients and process until they reached just the right note.

Keith and Pat sourced the seasonings and ingredients, knowing that, for now, their costs per chip were going to be relatively high because they weren't ordering in bulk. Once they increased the volume and scaled the business up, they'd be able to get the supply prices—and hence the profit margins—they needed. And by the end of 2006, after going over countless flavor and product possibilities, Keith and Pat had a final product they both loved: a thin, circular popped chip, in seven flavors. "It was," says Keith, grinning, "poptastic."

Bringing in the Branding Big Guns

As the food scientists worked out the details of the chip, Keith was also running parallel projects to create the name, graphic design, and personality of the brand. "In a competitive market like snacks, the branding and personality are just as important as the chips themselves," he explains. Plus he and Pat didn't have millions of dollars to spend on marketing and advertising like the corporate behemoths did. Instead, they'd have to be extra focused—and extra creative—to capture consumer interest from the get-go.

Keith had one, and only one, requirement for this new popped potato chip's branding: It had to be fun. "Fun! Fun! Fun! Fun!" he says. "We wanted to put the fun back into snacking. Snacking is an indulgence. It's not milk or salad or oatmeal. You want to enjoy it, eat the whole bag, and not worry about fat and calories. We wanted to have fun while still being fresh, different, and bold."

Keith set about the task of finding a design firm as if he were searching for the Holy Grail, interviewing everyone from the big powerhouses to the small boutique partnerships. "Seriously, people would laugh at me!" he says, smiling. "Ten, twenty, twenty-five firms . . . I just kept going. But I wanted to meet with people and see whose style resonated with me. You don't know what your design is going to be, but you can look at a road map of what people have done previously and get a sense of their aesthetic approach." He ended up with the small group Turner Duckworth, who later went on to do design work for Coke, Amazon, and Kraft. The group was based in both San Francisco and London, which was a big plus for Keith: He loved the visual appeal of UK packaging and wanted to bring a similar fresh feel to his chip brand.

This new popped chip company was in desperate need of something else: a name.

Just like with the design firms, Keith wasn't going to take any chances on missing the perfect name. So instead of hiring one great naming firm, he hired two! Their goal was to come up with something that Keith and Pat liked, that they could trademark, and that had an available URL (website address). Originally they were looking for a name like Epic Chips, and then the tag line would talk about the popped aspect, something like "popped potato chips." Keith and the firms spent over six weeks going down this path, looking at thousands (yes, thousands!) of names. But every time they found a name they all agreed on, they'd quickly come to a roadblock when it came to the trademark or URL. "There was literally not a single name where all three requirements came together," says Keith.

So they kept digging, trying all of the methods that the naming groups used to conjure up new directions. They were in yet another brainstorming meeting when the simplest idea came to Keith. He raised his hand, like a little kid broaching a guess to the grown-ups. "This is going to sound like a crazy idea, but what if we just call it Popchips?"

"It seems so obvious now, but we really needed to go through a process of brainstorming and clarification to get there," says Keith. "To the credit of both naming firms, they looked at me and said, 'Wow! That's a really interesting idea.'" One of the consultants rushed to the computer to do a quick URL search, and lo and behold, popchips.com was available. They didn't even have to see if any of the derivations commonly used to "cheat" a desired URL (say, popchipsnacks.com) were available instead—the literal URL was theirs for the taking. Everyone in the room started laughing. Things like this just didn't happen.

They immediately registered the URL, and then Keith called his lawyers to see about the trademark. He put a rush on the search and heard back the next morning; not only was the name available but it had actually been registered before and abandoned. Keith was ecstatic. Even if a trademark is available, there's no guarantee that the Patent and Trademark Office will approve it. But if Popchips had been previously approved and then abandoned, there was a high chance that it would get the official stamp of approval the second time around. It seemed like Popchips was meant to be.

A Personality-Driven Brand

Once he had a name, Keith needed a design. Turner Duckworth showed him five design prototypes, and he was immediately drawn to one. "It has certainly evolved from that initial sample, but I knew that I loved it the second I saw it," says Keith. The design used a black background with a burst of color for each flavor, so that a rainbow of Popchips would appear on grocery store shelves. But at the same time, each individual package looked smart and clean. Keith checked *design* off his list.

Next, Keith hired a copywriter to create the text on the package, a "terrific consultant" the design firm recommended. She spent hours interviewing Keith, then came back with three samples: each a completely different approach for how the brand's copy would declare its fun, wisecracking vibe. "I remember reading the second one and getting goose bumps," says Keith. "It captured everything I would've hoped for about this personality we were trying to achieve." Keith was even more excited when he saw that, on top of the package copy, she had also invented a "Snackers' Credo." "We, the snackers of the world, raising our right hands out of the chip bag, do solemnly pledge to engage in more recreational eating; to double dip into the onion dip as necessary; to throw more popcorn in the air to catch in our mouths; and to spoil our dinners on a regular basis. . . ." Keith was hooked. This was exactly what he was looking for. "Snacking is good and should be encouraged," continued the credo. Keith laughed. Popchips now had an identity.

"Snack. Smile. Repeat."

By early 2007, everything fell into place: Popchips had a name, a logo, an identity, a package, and a product. The finish line was seemingly in sight. But getting on retail shelves turned out to be just the starting point. "That's really where it all begins, because if it doesn't capture consumer attention, if it doesn't sell well, the stores will take you off the shelf," says Keith. Popchips had to figure out how to get that consumer attention, without the benefit of brand recognition or big money.

So instead of getting *on* that shelf, Keith put his focus on the other side of the equation: where (and how) could they best get Popchips *off* the shelf? What store, and placement, would make consumers most likely to buy a fun, better-for-you, all-natural chip? It was a strategic move, because an entrepreneur's first instinct is to just to get the product out there, on any grocery shelf. But Keith deliberately decided he wanted to launch Popchips at Safeway, the second largest grocery chain in the nation (after Kroger). Why? Because the company was also based in the Bay Area, and so Keith and his team could start at the local stores and use all of their personal connections to introduce their friends and acquaintances to Popchips. Keith's strategy was "one

WORD-OF-MOUTH BUZZ: FOOD TOUR EDITION

Bethia Woolf and Andy Dehus, the founders of Columbus Food Adventures, share the top lessons they've learned about running a successful local food tour business.

1. Create a memorable, professional brand. Starting a food tour business is a relatively low-capital endeavor, without the high start-up costs of something like a retail food operation. At most, you'll have to buy a used van and create a website. But because we're offering a service, not a product, looking professional is an extremely important part of being taken seriously. We put a premium on creating a logo and visual language so we looked official and established from the beginning. And your website becomes your public storefront—prioritize it! It's where the vast majority of our ticket sales are made, and it's the first experience most people have with us.

2. Build and maintain good relationships with restaurateurs. In a sense, the restaurants are your customers too; if they're not happy with the arrangement, you'll soon be looking for new material. You have to know the local restaurateurs—and the cheesemongers and bread makers and farmers and winemakers—to run a successful food tour. Before we started Columbus Food Adventures, we'd gotten to know a lot of people in the food community through blogging and volunteering at various events.

After a few years in business, it's easier to form new relationships because people have heard of us and we have a track record. You build those relationships by patronizing restaurants and producers, and you're researching and curating your tour at the same time. Being a good customer, interacting, and promoting local businesses (via word of mouth or social media) go a long way toward creating goodwill. You can't cold call or cold visit a restaurant and think they're going to trust you and be open to your tour.

You also have to be considerate of the restaurant. If you're just doing a traditional walking tour and staying outside, you can go any time of day and change things at a whim. But if you're going into restaurants and production facilities, you have to consider the best interests of everyone. You can't take a big group into a restaurant at 7 p.m. on a Friday night. We spend a lot of time setting up our tours around when our restaurants can accommodate groups; you can never just show up.

3. There's no such thing as a free lunch. Generally, food tour companies are paying restaurants for the food customers receive on a tour. While a tour *is* a type of promotion, it might not be enough to justify giving out free food. It's hard to know how many tour-goers will go back and patronize the restaurant, so plan on compensating a vendor just like any customer would.

4. Design great tours. There are lots of variables involved in this, including asking yourself, Is there enough food? Is there an interesting story or insider access? Is the food of exceptional quality or unique? Is the food provided in a logical progression? Do the individual tour stops provide enough material to allow the guide to tell a story? Do the individual stories gel into a larger, overarching story that defines the tour as a whole? Can the tour be conducted on foot or will van transportation be required? And offer a variety of tours. We've seen companies with just one tour to the big-name places, which limits your ability to get local customers and repeat business.

You also want to think about group size. How many people can comfortably fit into the restaurants and locations on your tour? What kind of atmosphere do you want? Can everyone hear you? In a crowded, noisy location, you may want a smaller group, like six to eight people. If you're going to larger production facilities you might be able to have a bigger group, like fourteen to sixteen people.

5. You're in the tourism business. Work with local visitors' bureaus and make sure to market to out-of-town visitors as well, such as people coming in for conventions, sporting events, and weekend getaways.

6. You're being evaluated. It's the age of Yelp, TripAdvisor, and Google, and that definitely carries over to food tours. Customers who have a good experience may take the time to say so on one of these review sites, but customers who have a bad experience are far more likely to vent their displeasure. It may not be fair, but it's just how it is. More than ever, you have to bend over backward to make unhappy customers happy.

7. Work the web. If your website is a storefront, then links and referrals are what drive customers directly to your doorstep. We put a high priority on search engine optimization (SEO): A lot of people are on Google looking for things to do, and you want them to be able to find you. It's also been important to generate incoming links through Twitter, Facebook, and bloggers. We haven't found much success with either print advertising or pay per click online advertising.

8. Word of mouth is the best advertising. We try to put on exceptional tours with great food, and we want to get credit for it. All kinds of print publications, blogs, and online magazines are looking for worthwhile content; if you're doing something great, why shouldn't it be about you? Reach out and let them know!

On the same note, word of mouth is incredibly powerful. It's unlikely you'll completely fill tours in your first few months of business. But even if you have only two people show up for a tour, give them the best experience possible. More than half of our customers say they heard about us from a friend, so every tour is really an investment in the future of your business.

snacker at a time," and he could do that only if he started in his own backyard.

Keith was able to leverage a few connections and get a meeting with a high-level executive at Safeway, where he pitched his new chips. He had a big plus going for him: Popchips was actually breaking new snacking ground. "For years, all of the innovation in the snack aisle had been about new kinds of fried chips and new kinds of baked chips: new flavors, new shapes, reduced fat this, reduced salt that," says Keith. "Nobody was telling a different story." So when Keith went in and talked about popped chips, with fun packaging and more healthful nutritionals, the interest level was high. So high, in fact, that Safeway wanted to launch Popchips nationally. But Keith was adamant; it needed to stay somewhat local, so he could create some grassroots buzz and get the word out through his own network. Remember, his goal was to get Popchips *off* the shelves, not just *on* the shelves. He and Safeway came to a solution—a larger launch than what Keith had originally wanted, but manageable—and in May 2007, they unleashed Popchips on the western United States.

The Greatest Launch Ever Told: Sixty Days in New York

The strategy worked. As the buzz spread, chip by chip, snacker by snacker, bags of Popchips started coming off the shelves (and then, of course, went back on the shelves). Keith and Pat gradually ramped up the business, but the real fun was just beginning. By early 2009, Keith was ready to move Popchips to the center of the universe and see if they could make it in Manhattan, without the benefit of all the local connections he'd had in California. As the saying goes, if he could make it there, he could make it anywhere. If that worked, then they'd expand to the whole Eastern Seaboard.

Getting Popchips into the hands of influential consumers had worked on the West Coast; could they do something similar in New York, without the same local roots? And while Popchips did have money to spend, they were also trying to compete with some of the largest, most well-funded food companies on the planet, like PepsiCo (which owns, through its subsidiaries, everything from Doritos to Stacy's pita chips). Keith had to think creatively: How could they create the biggest buzz for the buck? He decided to go all out for a short period of time, sixty days, so people would run into Popchips in all aspects of their lives: at events, at work, in stores, on the streets, and even at home. To make that happen, the bulk of Popchips's time and money would be spent on a grassroots-inspired, three-part sampling campaign.

How was Keith going to give out Popchips samples, face-to-face and person-to-person? He couldn't be everywhere at once, and he didn't have the same network he had in San Francisco. So Keith recruited not one but two of the best field marketing firms in New York, who go out to events and create a personal experience with a brand. His hunch was that getting actual Popchips into people's hands—the right people's hands—was far more important than advertising or traditional marketing. Then his new team pulled out their contact lists, got creative, and put the three pieces of Keith's sampling idea into play.

First up was the classic, broad-based sample giveaway. The Popchips team was soon handing out bags at Susan G. Komen races, charity parties in the Hamptons, and Mercedes-Benz Fashion Week. Keith had seen on the West Coast that while in-store demos worked well at places like Whole Foods and Costco, they fell flat at mainstream supermarkets like Safeway. What *did* seem to work was giving people a sample bag in other venues with information on where to buy more. So that's what they tried on the East Coast, handing out well over 250,000 bags of Popchips at targeted events in Manhattan.

The second sampling push was what Keith refers to as "the Influencer Campaign." "I wanted to focus on influencers—not necessarily famous or rich people, but that person who is cool, connected, and forward-thinking in his or her particular sphere," says Keith. He had talked to a few agencies across the country that develop influencer campaigns but came away thinking that he and the stellar field marketing teams he'd just hired could do it on their own, for less.

Keith broke the campaign into two parts: *the list* and *care packages*. First he needed to assemble a targeted list of influential New York tastemakers. "It wasn't about buying names, though," says Keith, "Because each individual we put on the list had to be a personalized contact, somebody on one of our teams had to know them, a one degree of separation thing." After they spent months creating the list—"I was a little crazy about it!" jokes Keith—they had a thousand names divided into categories such as hospitality, fashion, design, architecture, retail, finance, event planning, caterers, media, and fitness. Every hip enclave in the city was represented.

Then came the fun part. Twenty-five hundred New Yorkers were "popped" with a colorful care package box full of Popchips samples. Each kit also featured the pièce de résistance: a handwritten note, referencing the shared connection between Popchips and the recipient. "Hey Rachel, Keith thought you would enjoy these. Happy snacking!" the note would read—an incredibly personalized experience, replicating the effect of word of mouth among friends. Each box also included a "Pop It Forward card," so the recipient could go online and send the same care package to three of his or her friends, along with a similar note: "Hey Kathleen, Rachel thought you would enjoy these. Happy Snacking!" In effect, Popchips was making it extra easy for influencers to do what they do naturally—share new and exciting things in a viral fashion. And the results were nothing short of extraordinary; almost every influencer gifted Popchips to friends. As more and more people came home to a surprise box of Popchips, the buzz started to swell.

The third sampling strategy was what Keith calls *snack breaks*. He and the field marketing term put together a list of 200 companies in New York City where they had a "Popstar"—a fan or friend of the brand who would champion Popchips. Then the team showed up, baskets overflowing with bags of chips, for a snack break. There was always enough for every single employee, whether that was 25 people at an architecture practice or 650 at J.Crew corporate headquarters. "In every case, we had someone on the inside who would set it up and be our snack hero. That person would end up being quite popular!" says Keith. And they used their insider connection to deliver the samples in a personalized way for each spot: at a Monday morning strategy meeting at a design firm or in everyone's mailboxes at an Internet company.

Whew! On top of the monumental sampling approach, Popchips was ready to run a concentrated blast of advertising, smack dab in the middle of the sixty-day push. "We wanted to get some buzz building first, so people would start to recognize us," explains Keith. They took their sassy lines like "Love. Without the Handles" and put ads on the sides of buses and phone booths all around town. Then they launched with a strong retail presence at Duane Reade, the New York City drugstore that's on every corner—and is also very New York–centric—to align with Keith's localized approach. And the smaller efforts added up; Keith convinced several of their distributors to wrap their delivery trucks with pictures of Popchips. He dropped off boxes of Popchips for every radio DJ in Manhattan. On and on, everything the Popchips team could think of, they did in those legendary two short months.

And all of a sudden, just like Keith had hoped, people were saying, "Who are these guys? What is Popchips?" "During those sixty days, we were able to create a presence people still remember," says Keith. "I'll meet someone today and when I tell them I'm with Popchips, they say, 'You guys came out of nowhere. You must have spent millions of dollars on advertising!' I have to laugh, because we definitely did it on a grassroots, relatively modest budget for what we were trying to accomplish. But it worked. It really worked."

Just how well it had worked was soon to be clear in the numbers. Keith and Pat had set an aggressive sales target for their first year in New York, and Popchips hit it in less than six months. "We were thrilled with the response," says Keith. By the end of 2009, they had achieved more than double of what they'd hoped to and were in over 2,000 stores in Manhattan. As far as New Yorkers were concerned, they'd always known and loved Popchips. Naturally.

The Golden Ticket

Once Keith's localized, sixty-day plan was an unprecedented success in New York, he was ready to take it on the road. Throughout 2010 and 2011, he and his team took the buzz tour to fourteen more cities throughout the United States and Canada, and then to London in 2012. The personalized, over-the-top sampling approach was a golden ticket, and the sales numbers just kept growing: In 2008, Popchips's first full year, they sold about $6.5 million worth of chips. Just four years later, in 2012, customers around the globe bought almost $100 million of Popchips. Just as impressive as the sales was the Nielsen rating, which ranked Popchips as the fastest-growing potato chip brand in America.

As for Keith, his lunch routine has changed just a little. Now he picks up his sandwich and heads back to the office, where he chooses one of the latest flavors of Popchips to enjoy. "Sandwich. Meet your new B.F.F." goes the line in one of his ads, referring to best friend forever. Keith nods. "That's from personal experience!"

TAKE AWAY

- **Concentrate your efforts.** Create big buzz for your buck by strategically concentrating your marketing efforts in a short period of time and place, like the sixty days in New York City in Popchips's case. Whether it's geographic (like Boston) or thematic (like mothers who visit mommy blogs) try to canvas all aspects of the area and experience in a relatively short time frame so that repetition leads to recognition.
- **Work connections you never even knew you had.** When Keith prepared to invade New York, he called up the most connected people he knew and asked them to work *their* connections, growing his reach exponentially. Every Popchips team member brought his or her network to the table. Don't just ask who you know who can help with outreach, but who do *those* people know?
- **Target influencers who are in your larger network.** This doesn't mean Heidi Klum or the reality TV star du jour, but people within niche communities who are early adopter trendsetters. They're the ones who say, "You have to try this new x, y, z!" and stand in line overnight to get their hands on the latest iPhone. Your goals: Get your samples into the hands of these people, and give them an easy way to share it with their friends and acquaintances.
- **Surprise and delight.** Your product might be delicious and wonderful, but you want to make the experience special as well. When Keith sent the Popchips care packages out, they were unexpected, bright, and came with a personalized, hand-written note. In the current email age, that's an unusual delight. How can you surprise and delight your potential customers?

9

The Genius Financial Model

CAMERON HUGHES WINE

Wine aficionados Cameron Hughes and Jessica Kogan buy extra wine from high-end wineries and sell it under their own label for a fraction of the price. The result: premium drink meets everyday value.

An English Major Goes Rogue

Spend five minutes with someone in the wine industry, and they'll bring up their favorite joke. *Question: How do you make a small fortune in the wine business? Answer: By starting with a large one!* And as most clichés go, it's based in truth—except when it comes to Cameron Hughes and his wife, Jessica Kogan, who started their wine journey with no fortune to speak of. Then they quickly went from having no money to being in debt, not the direction they'd intended! But today, they own one of the largest wine companies in the United States and are a notable exception to the rule.

Cameron Hughes was born and raised in California's verdant

Ron Sellers

Cameron Hughes tastes a new Lot

agricultural hub, the Central Valley. Although his father, like many in the area, worked in wine, Cameron didn't see himself going into the business; he majored in English and philosophy in college. But Cameron's father didn't give up hope: To entice his son into the profession he himself loved, he'd often send mixed cases of wine to Cameron's dorm room. While Cameron grew to appreciate and love the vintages and varietals (and he and his friends enjoyed treating their palates to something a bit nicer than cheap college beer) he still considered wine a beloved hobby, not a career option. That is, until he graduated and found a nonexistent job market for English and philosophy majors. He set his sights on grad school and started taking classes to buff up his transcript, but when his father called with news of an easy part-time gig at value-priced label Corbett Canyon, Cameron jumped on it. If a job in his academic field wasn't in the cards, why not do something he really loved?

The job entailed going to retail stores and buying back any of the company's boxed wines that were past their expiration dates. Then Cameron would head to the backroom, slice them open, and dump the wine down the drain. "I wasn't making wine, selling wine, marketing wine, talking about wine; I was simply destroying wine," says Cameron. "But I was particularly good at it, I guess, so they soon offered me a job in sales." Grad school fell by the wayside, and Cameron was officially in the wine business.

Cameron spent the next four years as a sales associate for the brand, selling wines to large retail chains. But after a while he was itching to experience that more romantic side of wine again: tasting, evaluating, and sharing something he believed in—and selling big box wines to big box stores was not his idea of romantic. Who was doing something interesting in wine? That's where he wanted to work.

In quick succession, Cameron got jobs at two wine importing start-ups. Both companies tanked, but it was during his short time at each where Cameron learned all about the concept he would eventually use to launch his own business: *négociation*. The term refers to an old European business model of buying other vintners' excess inventory—everything from grapes to fermented juice to completed wines—then handling the rest of the process and selling the wine under the *négociant*'s own label. The start-ups were perfect examples: They didn't grow their own grapes, crush their own wine, or age their own juice, they'd just create blends from the high-quality leftover juice. "Then they'd bottle the wine, import it to the United States, and sell it," explains Cameron. "Or in their case, not sell it, which is why they crashed and burned. And fired me." But Cameron was intrigued. He looked around the California wine market; no one was doing anything like that with bulk wine. Could he be the first American *négociant*?

For the Love of Wine

While Cameron was learning the ins and outs of the *négociant* wine merchant business, he was also nurturing a long-distance relationship with fashion publicist Jessica (Jess) Kogan. It was a cross-country affair: He'd fly to New York, where they'd met, and she'd jet out to California. By the time the second start-up failed, he and Jess were officially serious. So when Cameron—fresh out of a job and with an idea burning a hole in his pocket—decided to start his own wine company, Jess was the first to jump onboard. "I'm sick of New York," she

Jake Westerfeld

Cameron Hughes and Jessica Kogan

said. "Why don't I just come out to San Francisco, and we'll do it together?"

Jess, who had helped launch Donna Karan's inaugural line and marketed luxury goods at various fashion dot-coms, brought her own expertise to the new venture.

But when she first told Cameron that she wanted to join him, he hesitated: "You have no experience in the wine business," he said. "But I do know what people like," reasoned Jess. "And I know how to make people like the things I believe in." As it turned out, the wine business was surprisingly similar to the fashion business: "They're just one DNA sequence apart," says Jess. "They're both about fantasy, perceived luxury, and perceived value. And whether in fashion or wine, you have to create those for the consumer." Cameron's wine knowledge combined with Jess's branding know-how was looking like a nice match. And with that, their little idea started taking on substantive shape.

In Search of Cinergi

Cameron's key idea was this: He and Jess weren't going to buy a vineyard. They weren't going to buy grapes or a winery. In fact, they weren't going to make their wine at all. They would instead focus on excess bulk wines, which were (and are) an open industry secret. Wineries have long made more wine than they need or plan on selling; they want various grape juice components on hand to create just the right blends or to ensure enough premium-level grapes for their brands.

Then came the era of cult status wines, where the asking price of some California vintages soared into the thousands of dollars. Part of the appeal was that these wines took extra care to produce (true) but also that there were a limited number of bottles on the market. So a small, famous winery in Napa Valley would release only *x* amount of bottles a year to keep demand higher than supply. But in any given year, that famous winery might have thousands of dollars' worth of wine left over after bottling. Some produced "second labels," distancing the wine from their higher-end lines. And some sold it to bulk wine merchants, who would mix the premium wines into barrels of low-end plonk to give it a little something-something.

And then came Cameron, with his *négociant* idea for bulk wine. At a dinner party, he noticed a friend struggling to finish an intense, pricey Zinfandel. Cameron had an outlandish thought: He reached for the other bottle on the table, a $10 red, and added a splash to the Zin already in the wineglass. The result was perfect: rich, but structured and infinitely drinkable. Blends like this were anomalies in a California market flooded with single varietal fruit bombs—and the offerings in the bulk market were similar. But what if Cameron bought single varietal bulk wines and then combined them, just as he had at the dinner table?

So in 2001, he and Jess started Cinergi (think synergy) Wines with the goal to make "funky, crazy" blends that had never been seen before. They bought some excess wine, mixed it together, and put their Cinergi label on it. Then they loaded up the trunk of Cameron's old Volvo and started going from wine shop to wine shop, where they met mild acclaim. But as they tried to sell their blends, which critics called "ahead of their time," all of Cameron and Jess's limited cash was tied up in the cases of wine sitting in their Volvo. When promising new bulk buys surfaced, there was no way to add them to Cinergi's inventory.

"It was a classic case of getting buried under the cash flow snowball," says Cameron. "We couldn't make enough money to reinvest in more inventory and grow the company. I still thought it was a great idea, but we couldn't make it work financially." By 2003, Cameron and Jess agreed they couldn't invest any more time, effort, or money in Cinergi; they needed to return to the corporate world and bring in some paychecks. Cameron went to work for some area wine companies, and Jess joined a team that was rebranding Chevron gasoline. Was this the end of their wine dream?

The Genius Idea: Lot Wines

In the meantime, Cameron and Jess made their business partnership official in another way: They got married in May 2003. Then, in the following January, their winemaker friend Samuel Spencer dropped by to see Cameron. "I've got this 2002 Lodi Syrah that I just can't sell," he told Cameron, referring to wine from a local region. "I have similar Napa Valley Syrah, with a 93 score from Robert Parker, that I sell for twice the price. But I can't move the Lodi stuff." Samuel was going to discontinue the Lodi program and double down in Napa. Could Cameron find a home for the remaining Lodi Syrah?

And that's just what Cameron did. The Syrah became the so-called Lot 1 of the brand-new, just-dreamed-up Cameron Hughes Wine Lot Series—limited-edition wines from famous, high-end wineries and regions, but sold at a fraction of the price. The catch? While the customer would see the grape type, year, and general origin of the wine, they wouldn't know the small, name-brand winery it came from. Instead, they'd have to trust this eponymous Mr. Cameron Hughes to pick the best of the best wine values. The idea was that the Cameron Hughes Lots would be an ongoing program—with its own brand recognition—instead of disparate one-off sales of bulk wine bottlings.

And when an outstanding wine was gone, it would be gone for

good. "Honestly, we were the original flash sale," says Cameron. "In 2005, I sold out of our Lot 17—500 cases' worth—in under two days. Now the business model is used with everything from fashion to art, but when we started it was still completely novel, especially in wine."

But back in January 2004, Cameron still had to get Lot 1, of which he'd just committed to buying about 800 cases, out the door. He called up every wine store and buyer he'd ever worked with, and got the same response: "Eh. Send a sample over, I guess." Finally, he cold-called the wine buyer at the local San Francisco Costco. "He didn't know me from Adam," says Cameron, who then dove into an explanation of why the Lot program was an absolute perfect fit for Costco: "It's a small buy. It's in today, out tomorrow. This is a total treasure hunt item." The buyer was interested enough to have Cameron bring by a sample, but he was leaving for Europe the next morning; it would have to be after he returned. Cameron wasn't willing to wait. "I set a land speed record driving from San Francisco to Livermore and dropped off a sample!" says Cameron. The next day the Costco buyer called from the airport. He would take everything they had. Lot 1 was really happening—a $28 Lodi Syrah selling for $8.99. Cameron and Jess were back in the wine business.

The Dynamite Business Model

Soon, their local Costco buyer, as well as the northern California regional buyer, was ready for more. Could Cameron Hughes Wine give them Lot 2—and beyond? Cameron and Jess masterminded a plan that would help them avoid the cash flow pitfalls they'd run into with Cinergi. They brought on a winemaker and together they'd come up with eight to ten samples crafted from the bulk wine market. Each was sourced only after the signing of nondisclosure agreements, and Cameron could never share exactly where each Lot had come from. Then Cameron and Jess would go into a meeting and present the wines, hinting at their storied pasts. The secret was that Cameron Hughes Wine hadn't purchased any of the offerings the Costco buyers were currently tasting; all of their samples were on spec.

It was only once the Costco buyers had chosen the wines they wanted to carry that the real fun began. Cameron and Jess would sprint out to the parking lot, one calling the wineries and the other their bank. While Cameron was saying "We'll take it!" to the winery, Jess was arranging financing, using the purchase order Costco had just made as collateral. The loaned money spent just seconds in the hands of Cameron Hughes Wine before it was transferred to the wineries and bulk wine merchants—and Cameron already knew a payment was on the way from Costco.

This solved that little cash flow problem they'd run into before. To grow the brand, they had to borrow, and spend, money only *after* they were already guaranteed a sale. In short, first they'd sell their wine and *then* they'd buy their supply. "It's actually the way the fashion industry works," says Jess. "You show your samples, get your orders, take your purchase order to a bank financier, and *then* you order your inventory and have it shipped in. It's a well-known model, but no one was applying it to wine." It was clear that Jess's fashion know-how was going to be a boon to their wine business, after all.

And instead of using these bulk wines as silver bullets to fix lesser blends, Cameron and Jess were the first to say exactly what they were doing, introducing the American consumer to the concept of *négociation*. "We openly confessed that we didn't make these wines, but that we were finding, sourcing, and marketing them," says Cameron. "It was our story. But before that, it'd been an insider type of knowledge."

Genius, right? "It wasn't genius at all," says Cameron. "We had no other choice. Let me remind you that Jess and I owed hundreds of thousands of dollars to the people who had invested in Cinergi. We figured that company was going to go belly up and we'd never be able to face our investors, who were mainly our family and friends, again. We had a very strong incentive to make something work."

A $30 Wine for $8.99

Cameron, Jess, and Costco all thought they had accidentally stumbled onto a great model and product, but they still needed to convince their would-be customers. A few days after Lot 1 hit shelves at the San Francisco Costco, Cameron and Jess went in to see how it was selling. They rolled their cart to the wine aisle and could barely tell which boxes were theirs: just the tops had been cut off, and they couldn't even see the bottles. Were customers really going to reach in and grab an unfamiliar product? No wonder the cases were full—not a single bottle was gone.

It took them only a few seconds to act. Jess pulled open boxes, filling her cart with Lot 1. And Cameron, who pretended he had nothing to do with the wine at all, started chatting with passing customers. "Wow! You've got to try this stuff. It's basically a $30 bottle of wine for $8.99," he'd tell them. It seemed like a no-brainer. People started putting a bottle or two in their carts. Within fifteen minutes, Cameron had sold about twenty-four bottles of wine. Whatever he had just done, it worked. "You need to plant your butt in this store," said Jess. "*That* is how we're going to make this work."

Jess, who had spent many afternoons shopping at warehouse stores trying all of the food samples from vendors, was a firm believer in product demos. Standing in the aisles and sampling was how people were going to learn about their wines, and luckily, it seemed like Cameron had a knack for it. They called the Costco buyer. Could they put a table up and stand in the store? "Why not?" came the reply. "I don't think we've done that with wine before, but give it a shot."

Cameron put on what he calls his "carnival barking act," selling the wine with everything he had. Customers would hear him all the way on the other side of the store and come over to see what was going on. Who was this guy, and what was he selling? "I had no credibility, no name recognition," says Cameron. "And I was basically swearing that this was incredible wine. So I'd back my promise with all sorts of collateral, like that if a customer didn't like the wine I'd go wash their car for free." (He never had to make good on the offer.)

The sales strategy worked, and soon Cameron was selling twelve cases, eighteen cases, and then a pallet (fifty-six cases) of wine a day. "I'm not kidding you. That's a ton of wine," says Cameron. "That's 720 bottles of wine times $8.99, which is over six grand of wine a day." Costco had never seen anything like it, either, and they most definitely wanted more and more Lots from Cameron Hughes Wine.

There's hard selling, and then there's hand selling, and the latter became an integral part of what made Cameron Hughes Wine unique. Soon, Costco was sending them out to demo in every store in the state, and Jess left Chevron to work full time on the business. She and Cameron would spend every Thursday through Sunday hawking wine at Costco. Then they'd devote Monday, Tuesday, and Wednesday to actually running the company: selling, buying, sampling wines, and taking care of logistics.

"It was crazy, and unsustainable," says Jess. They could keep it up for only so long. But then a guy named David, who was a big fan of the Lots, started chatting with Cameron during a demo. He was looking for a part-time job and had an idea. Could he help relieve Cameron on the store floor? Cameron was wary; until now, he'd been putting the personal Cameron Hughes magic touch into every sales pitch, and, well, this guy seemed a bit dorky. "Just let him try. It can't hurt. You can't keep standing at Costco four days a week," Jess convinced him. So they put David in a store and let him work his own brand of magic. Here was an everyday guy who loved Cameron Hughes Wine—it was a marketer's dream, and David made good on the premise. "David was so great, it became legendary!" laughs Cameron. "One Saturday he even sold 117 cases of wine, something we had never imagined."

If an employee could rack up numbers like that, then this demo idea could truly work. And Jess didn't stop with hiring a few salespeople. They were going to make their wine sampling service scalable, not just for Cameron Hughes Wine but for other wine and spirits brands as well. "The owners can't do it all themselves," she says. "Obviously, most sales people aren't as good as the owner of the company, but if you can get them to be 50 or 60 percent as effective and multiply that by a sales force of 500 people, you've more than made up for it."

Cameron Hughes Wine was running such a successful demo enterprise for their own line that other wine and spirits companies were willing to pay for a chance at the Midas touch. So over the past five years, Jess has grown that part of the business into its own separate company, Sales Pros. It manages in-store demonstration services for Cameron Hughes and other wine companies, holding wine tastings (wet demos) or simply talking about wines (dry demos). Today, that little spin-off idea that came out of the carnival barking act employs more than 500 people across the United States.

World Wine Web

Jess had another prescient requirement for Cameron Hughes Wine, picked up from her days in dot-com marketing: the wines needed to be sold online. So starting with Lot 1, Cameron Hughes had an e-commerce-enabled website (chwine.com). Jess was convinced that people would buy a $15 bottle of wine online, even though every industry and Internet expert was telling her otherwise. And by 2005, Jess was proving all of the naysayers wrong. If you marketed it (and kept shipping costs low) people *did* want to buy their affordable wines online. Lots regularly started selling out in forty-eight hours, and customers would pick up twelve or twenty-four bottles at a time. "Our online business is what kept us going for a long time," says Jess, "because that's where the greatest profitability was (and is)." Plus, it let Cameron Hughes Wine reach a market outside of California long before they had moved into physical stores across the country.

While the business of food is filled with lots of regulations and oversight during manufacturing, the business of alcohol is especially rife with regulations governing the sale and shipment of goods—especially when it comes to selling alcohol across state borders. Cameron Hughes Wine had to deal with the legacy of the Twenty-First Amendment, which broke up one American alcohol market into fifty different markets (we know them as, of course, states). "Each market is its own battleground, with its own rules and paperwork," says Cameron. Today, they can ship to thirty-seven states. But don't fear that there's a vast unconquered market in the remaining thirteen states—the thirty-seven allowed include 90 percent of the wine-drinking public. Only two states (Massachusetts and Pennsylvania) are left on their shipping wish list; the remaining no-ship states don't matter in their big-picture view. Like presidential candidates after electoral votes, Cameron and Jess instead focus their energy on the heavy-hitting states. That means California, New York, Texas, Florida, and Illinois, where the big sales (direct ship and in store) are made.

The Rise of Competition and a New Model

Once Cameron Hughes Wine was successfully buying, marketing, and selling premium bulk wines, it was only a matter of time before copycat competitors wanted in. While at first it seemed that Cameron and Jess had buttoned up the market, two events eventually opened the model up to competition. First was the unprecedentedly large harvest of 2005, which caught grape growers and winemakers off guard. Everybody had more grapes than they knew what to do with, and an abundance of supply came onto the bulk wine market. "It didn't change things initially, but it made people start to think about what they should do with all that excess wine," says Cameron. Suddenly, it wasn't a minor market but a large and potentially profitable one. As a result, things like Two-Buck Chuck, the Charles Shaw wine sold at Trader Joe's, began to come down the pipelines.

But Cameron Hughes Wine didn't see true direct competition until after the financial meltdown in 2008, when consumers simply stopped buying expensive premium wines. High-end wineries began to struggle and ask, "How do we sell this wine and at least break even, instead of selling it at a loss?" One solution was the private label brands that started to pop up and quickly became the go-to solution for excess and unsold wine. Most riffed on the Lot concept that Cameron had introduced so successfully, marketing the wines as limited and special purchases. Then the flash sale websites, like WineShopper and Lot18, surfaced to take advantage of the recessionary wine glut. "But now that true distressed wine inventory is gone, and they're all struggling," says Cameron. "Today I saw a deal site selling a $65 bottle of wine for $59. Why would I buy that from you?" The difference, he says, is that Cameron Hughes Wine was never just about distressed inventory, the easy pickings that you just slap a label on and sell. Instead, the idea was to use their relationships to source the bulk wine deals that have always been available, good economy or bad.

And today, Cameron Hughes Wine isn't struggling because when the competition started to appear, Cameron and Jess shifted their own model just slightly. Now the company essentially owns its full supply chain, but in an outsourced, *négociant*-inspired way. And so while other private labels and flash sales are left scrounging for bargain finished wine, Cameron can find excess and glut opportunities at every step of the wine-making process, from vineyard space to ripe grapes to blending facilities.

Over the years, as the stream of bulk wine has both flowed freely and dried up, Cameron has sought to secure a constantly larger supply. And as a result, the Cameron Hughes Wine team has moved into what they call "virtual wine making." First, Cameron Hughes leases empty wine barrels (which can cost upward of $700 apiece new). Then they find wineries or growers with excess production capacity—not that they've grown too many grapes or made too much wine, but that they *could* grow or make more if there was a right-priced market for it.

The wineries with excess production capacity go out and source and buy grapes on Cameron's behalf and sell them to Cameron Hughes Wine by the gallon. "Then we bring our barrels and winemakers to the party, and we make the wine together," says Cameron.

THE KICKSTARTER ROCK STARS

A couple creates a healthier version of microwave popcorn, then raises $30,000 in financing on Kickstarter, an online funding platform for creative projects, to turn their dream into a reality.

FROM BABY QUINN TO POPCORN QUINN

In December 2010, Kristy and Coulter Lewis came home from the hospital with their first child, Quinn, and immediately jumped into . . . Quinn Popcorn. Kristy's three-month maternity leave was a chance to run with their idea of making an all-natural microwave popcorn, one without the chemical-coated bags conventional versions rely on. Their goal was to see if this popcorn business was worth pursuing full-time, so Kristy spent her child's first ninety days constantly on the phone and computer. "Luckily, Quinn was the best baby ever, so I could do that," she says. "If he hadn't been so well behaved, there wouldn't be any Quinn Popcorn!" adds Coulter.

As the end of her leave neared, Kristy and Coulter took a good look at what she'd found: A product and technique that worked and the beginnings of relationships with the right suppliers. It was enough to make them think that maybe, just maybe, this could happen. So Kristy called up her boss, told him about the popcorn project, and went out on her own. From then on, it was nonstop Double Quinn: As Kristy discussed logistics with suppliers, manufacturers, and designers, she'd tuck baby Quinn in his stroller and take long walks, dialing away. Within a few months, they had boxes full of their new microwave popcorn and huge, looming bills from vendors.

THE KICKSTARTER SOLUTION

Coulter and Kristy had spent a significant amount of their savings on the popcorn project. When asked how much, Coulter jokes, "All of it." Their grand total came to about $30,000. But now they needed more than money—they also needed to get the word out about a company that was, until this point, completely secret. The couple knew about Kickstarter.com and were active participants, donating to a variety of projects from a musical group to a guy who made cast iron cookware. "We were already enamored with the idea of it, so going to Kickstarter wasn't a Eureka! moment, it just felt like a no-brainer," says Coulter.

The couple realized that there are different kinds of campaigns on the site, from full-on philanthropy to simply buying a product from a start-up. They fell somewhere on the middle of the spectrum—half do-good, half start-up. "If you said 'I'm going to pre-sale this product at an incredible premium,' it wouldn't make any sense for a consumer. But that's why Kickstarter is so magical: People want to help out," explains Coulter. For example, a pack of Quinn Popcorn that went for a $15 donation during the Kickstarter campaign would retail for $6 today ($10 with shipping). So for each $15 order, about $5 of the price could be considered a pure donation.

Kristy and Coulter knew they'd need more than a fast plea to succeed on Kickstarter; they'd have to create a whole campaign, including a video and a reward structure. "Kickstarter was our chance to tell everyone what we were doing in a big way," explains Coulter. "And that's why the video was so important, because we wanted to share not just *what* we were doing, but *why*." They took over two hours of footage to create their final thirty-second clip. Then they set up a reward structure ranging from $5 to $500. For example, $5 would get you a postcard; $15 would get a box of the popcorn; and $500 would result in a yearly subscription of all three Quinn flavors.

KICKSTARTER TAKE OFF

Kristy and Coulter set their fundraising goal for $10,000 and went live. "It was terrifying," remembers Coulter. "We had no idea how it would go. Thirty seconds after we pressed submit, we were wishing we'd set our goal for $2,000." (On Kickstarter, you get the pledged money only if you reach or exceed the goal you set at the beginning.)

Kristy looked at her phone the second she woke up the next morning and thought there had been a glitch with Kickstarter. Had they really made $1,000 overnight? They were ecstatic and amazed, and their euphoria only increased during the thirty days the campaign was live. "The feedback we got was off the charts, and it wasn't simply from friends or family; we didn't tell anyone we knew until a few days in because we were worried our campaign would be a bust," says Coulter. But because of that, they also found that Kickstarter brings its own audience. In the end, Quinn Popcorn had 755 backers who collectively donated $30,000. They'd also received an abundance of press and recognition. Thanks to their phenomenal success on Kickstarter, they were able to expand just as Quinn's—both the boy and the popcorn—first birthday rolled around.

Want to learn more? Kristy and Coulter documented their whole start-up story at quinnpopcorn.com.

It's win–win: it lowers the wineries' per-bottle overhead cost, allowing them to keep a more experienced staff on year round and to obtain better pricing on grapes.

Once Cameron figured out what makes wineries tick, he started going to grape growers too. "We love your fruit," he says. "What if we partnered you up with a high-end custom facility and we all make wine together in a triangular contract?" Cameron's goal is to engineer a system of mutually beneficial agreements so that he doesn't pay for a drop of wine until it comes out of the barrel (it's analogous to his strategy of buying the bulk wine *after* selling it to Costco). By bringing growers, wineries, and Cameron Hughes Wine together, he could maintain a positive cash flow. (It's a common business tenet; similar strategies exist at places like Costco and Walmart, where manufacturers and companies aren't paid until, or after, their product actually sells.)

Cameron found high-quality growers across the state who would gladly do business with him and carry the cash flow obligation of the deal. "We can control the style, the direction, and the quality of the wine," he says. "But financially, it's like a bulk wine deal in that we don't pay for it until it's ready to go into the bottle." Most of the deals also have nondisclosure agreements attached to them, and as a general rule, Cameron Hughes Wine doesn't say who they're working with. But now they don't have to wait for the once-in-a-lifetime bulk wine buys; they can create their own. "This is how the Europeans have been doing it for centuries," says Cameron. "It's just a modern evolution of the California wine business."

Growing Beyond Costco

Obviously, Costco was a boon for Cameron Hughes Wine; from day one, Lot 1, its buyers were incubating the company. And by 2007, Costco was also the largest retailer of wine in the *world*—and not just in value wine but in fine wine, too. But, eventually, Cameron knew he had to build the brand beyond Costco's walls. "It's a great place to start, but it's also a risky proposition," says Cameron. Costco doesn't want a company to have all their eggs in one basket: The buyers are continually rotating products, and they're well aware that if they drop you for a cycle, you'll likely go out of business. "They *wanted* us to have other accounts," explains Cameron. But he and Jess found that it was a tremendous challenge to grow outside of Costco. First, they had to convince other retailers, who didn't want to compete with the bargain-priced behemoth down the street, that it could work. And second, they needed to increase their inventory dramatically because Costco would immediately take the majority of what Cameron Hughes Wine could find and finance.

To solve the conundrum, Cameron Hughes Wine would need to increase their credit limit so they could finance more wine. Their solution was to take on a large, high-interest loan for a short period of time, which acted as collateral and let them secure a larger credit limit from their main bank. With that in place, they built their inventory up to a five-month supply—enough so that they could guarantee a continued selection of Lots to other stores, not just Costco. "Then we went out and scorched the earth. It's taken years, but we've finally built a really healthy business outside of Costco," says Cameron. "Today, if there's a place you can sell wine, we're there. And it's sustainable."

Marketing Magic in a Bottle

Today, Cameron Hughes Wine is selling over *6 million* bottles of wine a year. How are they getting the attention of so many customers, when they've never run a single advertisement and have a marketing budget that covers just their demos and meet-and-greets? "Our goal has always been to let the wines speak for themselves, and then our customers will speak for us," says Jess. It's all about the grassroots power of word of mouth: people tell their neighbor about a great Cameron Hughes wine, and maybe gift a friend or family member a bottle or two. "Plus we know how to talk about wine, and we're passionate about where our wines come from," says Cameron. "We know the quality, and we know what other people sell them for. It's easy to benchmark it, like in our original $30 wine for $8.99 line."

One benefit of their low-overhead business model is that they're able to essentially put their advertising and marketing budgets straight into the actual product. Customers want a $40+ bottle of wine to *feel* expensive, which means heavy glass bottles with fancy labels and corks and marketing campaigns to create an aura of luxury. "But we don't need the exterior of our bottle to market our wine," says Cameron. "We buy cost-effective glass that costs half the price of other guys' glass. We buy cost-effective, fantastically well-made corks that cost a tenth of other guys' corks because I don't care what they look like. Our labels are classy, but they're inexpensive." Because their total product cost is relatively low, they don't have to hire advertising agencies and convince customers that the wine is worth it—at this price, people will try a bottle for themselves.

Cameron calls their strategy "foxhole-to-foxhole marketing": They convince one customer, and one store buyer, at a time. "It's still a handshake business, a relationship business," says Cameron. "There are tens of thousands of different wine brands now, and people want to know you're real. The retailers want to have a relationship with you. People always come up to me and go, 'Oh! There's a real Cameron Hughes? I thought that was a made up name.' That's how you sell wine once. To sell it again, it has to be worth it."

So You Want to Be Like Cameron?

Ah, but first you have to remember the cardinal rule of the industry: How do you make a small fortune in the wine business? By starting with a large one. "Anyone can get into the wine business with a little bit of capital," says Cameron. "But then you have to actually *sell* the wine, which can prove difficult." For the long term, he believes it's easier to start at the bottom in the industry and work your way up. Then you can build the contacts you'll need in this relationship-driven, handshake-based business.

But then, whether you're flush in cash or relationships, make your wine the way Cameron does—virtually. "Don't go buy land, grow grapes, and build a winery; it'll suck up more cash than you ever thought possible," he says. Instead, source your grapes and/or wine and give your venture a try first to see if it flies. "I think that's one of the only ways for a start-up to actually be profitable in wine . . . we got lucky. I found the right buyer at the right time at the right place, and I was holding the right bottle of wine. That's it," says Cameron. "There's a certain amount of initiative involved in that, but at the end of the day, the stars were aligned." And, one might say, a genius financial model helped keep those lucky stars in action.

TAKE AWAY

- **Consider cash flow in the beginning.** Be wary of tying up your limited cash in large amounts of inventory before you have a track record of sales. Work with small-batch prototypes as much as possible, so you can pivot and be nimble as new opportunities arrive.

- **Borrow—and spend—money only after you're guaranteed a sale.** Jess and Cameron applied the fashion industry model to wine, using their purchase order as collateral on a loan and then using that loan to pay their suppliers. Can you wait to make large amounts of product until after you have a purchase order? Or will suppliers work in tandem with you, supplying raw ingredients while you handle manufacturing and sales?

- **Keep overhead and advertising spending low.** If you operate on a lean and mean budget, you can make a value-priced product and skip the advertising and marketing it takes to sell a premium-priced item. Then put *that* money into creating or sourcing a great product, and grassroots and word-of-mouth marketing will move it off shelves—every consumer loves a secret value find.

10

Selling Luxury

VOSGES HAUT-CHOCOLAT

Katrina Markoff infuses luxury truffles and chocolate bars with the exotic flavors and stories of her globetrotting adventures.

The Rules of Fine Cooking

As Katrina Markoff starts to conjure up her beguiling chocolate tale, she looks exactly like you'd expect a bohemian jetsetter to—with her mass of wavy brown hair and signature chandelier earrings, her vibe is half free spirit, half old money luxury. But for all of her worldliness today, Katrina's childhood in Indiana was remarkably ordinary. Her mother, Michelle, took on a janitorial supplies sales job after her divorce, which she eventually built into a successful waste management business. As the family's finances stabilized, Michelle slowly filled her closet and home with heirloom, well-made European pieces. All the while, she was passing on two concepts to her daughter that would crystallize years later: a penchant for entrepreneurship and a deep appreciation for handcrafted, thoughtful, high-end goods.

Katrina picks up her own story on the day she graduated from Vanderbilt in 1995, armed with dual degrees in chemistry and psy-

Chris Fanning

Katrina Markoff

chology and a ticket to Paris, where she would enroll in Le Cordon Bleu culinary school. She followed that up by securing a pastry job at a grand old restaurant, prepared to crème patisserie her way into the finest kitchens in France. But after months spent creating exacting and formalized desserts, Katrina was frustrated; she'd come to learn the rules, but her days in a windowless, utilitarian kitchen were sapping her creativity.

Then a friend suggested they leave behind the chilly streets of Paris and move to Spain, where they could apprentice at an emerging mecca of the culinary world, El Bulli. And as each day passed, Katrina started to put aside the culinary edicts that had been the mainstay of codified French cuisine—the hierarchical order, the crisp white jackets, the "right" way of saying hello in the morning. Instead, chef Ferran Adrià was breaking the rules in a big way, which was just the sort of revolutionary thinking in which Katrina reveled. In lieu of dark walls, there were picture windows overlooking gardens. Chef uniforms were out; everyone wore jeans and aprons. And instead of executing a limited repertoire of tired, classic dishes and ingredients, the chefs were using their imaginations and creating new, wondrous combinations. Katrina loved it. So when Ferran suggested she skip the internship tour through Europe's great restaurants and instead travel and let her palate guide her across cultures, Katrina listened; she bought an around-the-world plane ticket and headed east.

A Taste for Travel

Over the next nine months, Katrina followed her taste buds as she journeyed to Thailand, Vietnam, Singapore, Hong Kong, Korea, and Australia. "It was a deep dive into these fascinating indigenous food cultures," says Katrina. "I was meeting people, eating every new, exotic food, working in restaurants, going to cooking classes, and visiting people's homes for meals and straight-from-grandmother culinary wisdom."

In the floating markets of Bangkok, for example, Katrina tried limes and chiles that were grown in tiny backyard gardens. In Vietnam, she saw chickens slaughtered to order, their blood spurting all over. Everywhere she went, Katrina took notes on flavor combinations and pairing ideas, thinking of the dishes she'd create someday. But when she returned to her childhood home in Indiana, the career plans that had seemed so promising abroad didn't materialize. Without a plan, and, quite frankly, broke, Katrina pondered her future. Had her whirlwind adventure been for naught? In the meantime, her uncle had recently started his own mail-order furniture company, and he needed administrative help. Did Katrina want to come down, just to earn some money? The twenty-three-year old trained chef, chemist, and world traveler didn't think twice. The year was 1997, and she was headed to Texas.

The Magic of Storytelling

Katrina's uncle John Himelfarb had worked for years in the mail-order division of high-end stalwart Neiman Marcus, creating evocative catalogs to entice and delight customers. He was planning to do the same with his new home decor business. While Katrina had thought she'd just be filing papers and handling customer calls, she was instead about to receive an immersion course in luxury sales and marketing.

As he sourced items and created catalogs, John taught Katrina the importance of pairing a story with the actual physical merchandise. She learned that you can't just list an opulent blanket, bed, or handbag for sale; you have to take a beautiful photo and then write text that romanticizes the item and explains why it's worth so much money. You delve into the background of where and how it was made and talk about the special, precise details. The goal is to connect the customer to the product, so when they see a price tag and say, "What? A thousand dollars for *that*?" there's an explanation and reason.

When John started putting together his holiday catalogs, he made an off-hand remark as he mused over the lineup: "We should get some great food items for the fourth-quarter books, because people buy a lot of specialty treats during the holidays. It would be nice to add to the mix." Katrina started searching for gourmet chocolates, cheeses, and cookies at trade shows and wholesale markets. But despite the seeming abundance of choices available, there was nothing she wanted to feature among John's high-end, innovative furnishings. "To my palate, everything I found tasted terrible; it was saccharine sweet, with no flavors except insipid nut pastes and runny cherry fillings," says Katrina. Plus each package touted a similar story: grandmother's recipe for this, grandmother's recipe for that. "It was like nothing had changed about chocolate since World War II!"

While all of this whirled in her head, Katrina's cupboards were stocked with spices, dried herbs, roots, and flower petals she'd picked up on her travels. She also had stacks of notes and recipe ideas. So one night she picked up blocks of chocolate and heavy cream at the store and started playing around in her kitchen. As usual, Katrina was wearing one of her favorite necklaces, a strand of tiger's teeth from the Nagaland tribe in India. She had received it as gift in Hong Kong and found its unknown origins bewitching. She started whisking up chocolate truffles, drawing on a few days of chocolate-making classes she had taken in Paris. All the while, Katrina kept fingering her necklace and thinking about the Nagaland people. Into the milk chocolate ganache went sweet curry powder and shredded coconut, ingredients she associated with Naga cooking. Soon Katrina had a tiny Naga-inspired chocolate ball. She immediately christened it Naga and took a bite. "Finally, here was a chocolate I loved tasting," she remembers.

Katrina had her epiphany: What if she used chocolate as a medium to tell stories about her travels, the cultures she'd seen, the religions she'd learned about, and all of the fantastic flavors she had experienced? She believed there was a market for innovative chocolate: Americans were just becoming interested in things like artisan wine, beer, and coffee, and she was willing to bet that chocolate would be next. It was the right place at the right time, and Katrina could suddenly see all of the disparate parts of her life come together.

Katrina stayed up all night, ultimately creating twenty different truffle recipes. Each used exotic, unexpected ingredients and was given a transporting story and an evocative name. Her chocolates crisscrossed the globe, from the Black Pearl made with ginger, wasabi, and sesame seeds to the Budapest, which was subtly flavored with zesty Hungarian paprika. "I had personal experiences with all of these ingredients and countries, so in my head the combinations just came together naturally," she says. And thus was born her philosophy: Travel the World through Chocolate.

The next day, still high from her exuberant realization and night of invention, Katrina marched into the office with a tray of her truffles. "But this was barbeque-loving Dallas. Everyone was afraid to eat them!" remembers Katrina. A coworker skeptically reached for a truffle, ready to spit it out if it was as horrid tasting as it sounded. Her emotions cascaded across her face as she took a bite: first fearful, then surprised, and finally delighted. "I can't believe I like it! Let me try another one!" she enthused. Soon, the whole group was sampling. The fact that familiar chocolate was part of the deal made them more willing to try some of the crazier things Katrina had added. They were fascinated—and wanted more. "This is so powerful!" thought Katrina. "Chocolate can open people's minds." The chocolates combined everything from the handcrafted ethos she'd learned from her mother to her French culinary skills, globetrotting adventures, and luxury marketing experience. Katrina knew she had found her career.

Katrina, the Chocolatier

Soon after, Katrina reconnected with her childhood friend Julie Lang. Julie was now living in Chicago and had just what Katrina's fledgling chocolate venture needed—a business background. What if they worked together? Julie was interested, and Katrina was ready to return to her native Midwest. In early 1998, she quit her job and moved to Chicago, where she rented an apartment with enough room in which to make, package, and store the chocolates in. There were no business plans or forecasts, just a day-by-day attempt to see if this chocolate idea could work.

Katrina's mother agreed to pay the rent so her daughter could devote her time to creating a brand identity: Katrina's catalog work had taught her about the importance of design, logos, and packaging and especially about creating a sense of luxury and worth. Katrina's fledgling brand also needed a name, and she knew exactly the moment that would lend inspiration. Surprising for someone who was about to devote her whole life to chocolate, Katrina hadn't even liked the treat as a child. It wasn't until a meal in Paris, at a restaurant called L'Ambroisie in the Place des Vosges, that her perception changed.

The waiters there brought over a special little dish called a truffle beignet, which they wanted the enthusiastic Katrina to taste. The chef had taken chocolate ganache, frozen it in tiny balls, dipped them in batter, and then fried them. "When I popped a hot little bite into my mouth, the chocolate explosion was the most amazing thing I'd ever tasted," remembers Katrina. For the first time she realized how delicious, decadent, and interesting chocolate could be. As she began to invest all of her energy into her new business, she would return to that first transcendent experience. "I wanted to commemorate that moment. But when I lived in Paris, I could never say Place des Vosges correctly [it's pronounced *plas de vozh*]," she says with a laugh. "It doesn't sound like it should! But then I realized it didn't matter how people pronounced it." She added on *haut chocolat* as a play on haute couture, the term for exclusive luxury fashion; Katrina wanted her chocolate to be at that same high level. And voilà! Vosges Haut-Chocolat was officially born.

To cover their costs, Katrina and Julie each put $15,000 into a figurative pot that they'd use to run their business (Katrina borrowed the money from her mother). Soon the friends were able to get a $30,000 loan, using Julie's stocks as collateral. They kept their expenses as low as possible, and Katrina made everything out of her apartment. "I wasn't even aware of things like health regulations or shared commercial kitchens," she says. "We just went completely under the radar."

They bought packaging supplies from an outfitter that had been making the same traditional supplies—boxes, ribbons, candy cups, candy pads, and stickers—for over a hundred years. "They were so unattractive and unoriginal!" says Katrina. But they could afford only stock packaging because they'd have to place a very large order to qualify for customization. Then she made friends with the graphic designer at her local Kinkos, who taught her how to use the design software system Quark. He helped Katrina design catalog booklets, and another friend assisted with Vosges's first website. Katrina hand-drew the Vosges logo, and she and Julie printed off their booklets at Kinkos, cutting the pages and stapling everything themselves.

Katrina had developed her flavors, made the chocolates, and designed the packaging. So she set out, planning to go from store to store in the chic Bucktown neighborhood and take orders. She first walked into a high-end liquor shop, announcing, "Hi! I'm selling chocolates!"

The bored salesperson eyed Katrina. "Do you have a sell sheet?" she asked. Katrina looked down at the stack of business cards and samples she was carrying, which was all she had with her. She soon learned that she needed to go into a store armed not just with samples but with price lists, minimum purchase requirements, and sell sheets that detailed her story and products. "And then, most important, I had to sell my story," says Katrina.

Katrina's background—the apprenticeships in famous kitchens, far-reaching travels, and crazy things she'd tasted—made buyers stop and listen. Then, once they tried her chocolates, they realized that she was doing something new, unexpected, and delicious. Soon, she landed an account at Neiman Marcus and a few small accounts at various specialty food shops around Chicago. Although fusion chocolates would become the norm over the ensuing decade, it was an entirely novel concept in 1998, and Katrina was a forerunner of the high-end, small-batch, gourmet chocolate business. She was bound to get noticed, and if her avant-garde creations didn't scare off chocolate lovers, then success would follow.

That's when a piece of extreme good fortune hit: A *Food & Wine* writer had heard about Vosges and wanted to feature them. "I will always remember the day that story came out," says Katrina. "I was still making chocolates by hand in my apartment, and we'd barely even received any local press. We were just about to open our first little store in Bucktown, and all of a sudden we had orders pouring in from around the country and people *knew* about us."

Shortly thereafter, buoyed by the *Food & Wine* success, Vosges added a Magnificent Mile location on the famed Michigan Avenue shopping stretch in Chicago. At the same time, Katrina looked around and saw that the chocolate bar market consisted of Hershey's, Hershey's, and, oh yes, Hershey's. "Just like you couldn't get interesting, good truffles, you couldn't find good chocolate bars. I was lucky because the field was totally wide open. No one was telling any story or doing anything new," she says. So Katrina took an obvious-to-her step and put the truffle flavors into bars. While the new Vosges boutiques were the perfect way to display and spotlight $3 truffles, the new $7.50 bars (like Mo's Bacon with hickory smoked bacon, milk chocolate, and sea salt) would be Vosges's big volume hitters. Eventually, they would land in thousands of stores and introduce luxury chocolate to the everyday American consumer.

A Lesson in Luxury

As Katrina developed Vosges, one aspect was nonnegotiable: She wanted it to be a luxury brand. While she was at Le Cordon Bleu, Katrina and her mother spent blissful days visiting the renowned high-end Parisian haunts. From the original Chanel apartment on rue Cambon to the stunning stores of Louis Vuitton and Dior, they whiled away hours touching textiles and learning to appreciate the highest quality. "The salespeople would tell you all about their product, explaining how it was made and why it was worth the number on the price tag," explains Katrina. "And I was left with a deep reverence for beautiful, well-crafted items."

Katrina wanted to position her chocolate brand like couture fashion companies positioned theirs: as a brand that sold limited-edition items in high-end department stores and boutiques. The truffles were the couture of the chocolate world, and they were naturally limited. Without preservatives, which Katrina's restaurant training made her abhor, they would last a couple of weeks at most. (At the time, most other chocolates on the market, even so-called high-end ones, were packed with preservatives and could sit on a shelf for years.)

Katrina knew that, by definition, a luxury good would never have the same level of grocery store distribution as a mass-market product. Instead, she would have to be creative and use e-commerce, partnerships, and select retail opportunities to sell her chocolates. And she would have to consider every detail of the customer's experience—not just the chocolates themselves, but everything from the stunning photography and heavy weight of the paper in the catalogs to the online navigation of the website and the feeling the customer got when walking into a Vosges boutique.

As she worked, Katrina was constantly channeling brands like the legendary Parisian purveyor Hermès. Even their packaging is part of the ultimate luxury experience. "People collect those beautiful orange boxes and line them up in their closets," she says. "I hope it's the same thing with our Vosges boxes; we put as much effort into designing these gorgeous, limited-edition boxes as we do with the chocolate itself."

While developing her brand, Katrina envisaged a muse (she called her Sophie), the woman who was buying Vosges. Where did she eat? What designers did she wear? Where did she shop? The detailed answers to those questions helped Katrina set the tone of the brand and determine where she wanted to get Vosges on the shelves—wherever her idealized customer was.

Katrina also kept Sophie in mind as she created Vosges's standalone shops, which were of course modeled after high-end fashion boutiques. The stores aren't just blank spaces for buying chocolate, but lush environs that are meant to be as decadent and experiential as the chocolates themselves. The walls are bathed in deep purple (a color theme that's carried out everywhere from the boxes to the pens used to sign credit card receipts) and crystal chandeliers hang from the ceilings. Ornate, velvet-covered chairs invite patrons to relax with a wine-and-chocolate tasting flight. And Katrina's hope is that customers will immerse themselves in the world of chocolate, from touching cacao pods to viewing pictures of Belize, where some of Vosges's cocoa beans are grown.

New York, New York

By 2001, Katrina and her partner, Julie, decided to part ways. Suddenly Katrina was on her own, and she knew exactly what she wanted the next step for Vosges to be: a New York City flagship store. Shortly after 9/11, Katrina found a space on Spring Street in SoHo, a prime spot that a friendly landlord decided he would rent to her for (just) $18,000 a month.

At the time, Vosges wasn't yet profitable; every penny of revenue was poured back into growth and salaries (including a below-market salary for Katrina). Katrina was sure that her financial and legal team would never sign off on a new, seemingly extravagant location (the rents on the Chicago shops were only $1,000 and $5,000, making the $18,000 for the SoHo spot seem even more astronomical). "So I just signed the lease, without telling anyone," explains Katrina. "Why should I? It was my company. And when I told them, everyone thought I had made a huge mistake."

But when the SoHo boutique opened, it changed the entire game. "So much of the national and international media is based in New York, and they just ate it up. Everyone—*everyone*—covered it because they'd never seen anything like the chocolates or the boutique before," she says. It sparked growth across the entire brand. Soon Vosges bars were being distributed in hundreds of Whole Foods locations, and the New York store was overflowing with both locals and tourists. Katrina was even able to purchase an environmentally friendly, LEED-certified production plant/corporate headquarters outside of Chicago (which she outfitted with perks like a yoga and meditation room). "It all happened because the media is an incredibly powerful way to reach people," she explains. And for the very first time, Vosges ended the year with a profit.

Chocolate + Partners = Success

As she grew Vosges, Katrina wanted to ensure that her chocolate never existed in a bubble; she envisioned it as part of a holistic lifestyle, marrying things like wine, yoga, beauty, fashion, music, and architecture. "The idea is to get as many touch points—ways that people can experience Vosges besides simply going to a store and buying chocolate—as possible," she explains. Partnerships are a big part of that philosophy: Vosges has done yoga and chocolate events, which represent the spiritual side of chocolate. They've collaborated with up-and-coming fashion designers, selling special limited editions of the designer's clothing or handbags in Vosges boutiques. They created a line of healthy, antioxidant-rich chocolates with beauty maven Bobbi Brown and hosted a chocolate and music pairing, where each piece of chocolate was experienced with a specific song.

Katrina explains that such partnerships come about in all sorts of organic ways when you're actively looking. For example, Bobbi Brown's store is near the Vosges SoHo location, and so she'd often drop by and pick up chocolate. Then Vosges's publicist Natalie Markoff (Katrina's sister) was chatting with Bobbi's publicist one day, and the whole thing took off from there. Or someone will just read about Vosges in the press and reach out about a possible collaboration. "Our attitude is to be open to anything," says Katrina. "As I like to say, with what would chocolate not marry? Very little!"

"If You're Not Evolving, You're Dying."

Today, with an internationally recognized luxury brand—and one that's still rapidly expanding—does Katrina feel like she's achieved the dream? "I was lucky when I started," she says. "There was no one in this space. In a way, it was easy: Customers, store buyers, and the media *wanted* to talk about what I was doing. I just needed to keep executing." But these days, there's substantially more competition with local and artisanal chocolate makers, and she's continuously challenged to stay on her toes and create new space for Vosges in the market. Katrina laughs, saying, "I'm never done! If you're not evolving, you're dying."

Katrina's vision for the future is to create a fully vertical business, where Vosges does everything from growing cocoa beans and making the chocolate base to selling the finished products in stores: "bean to bar, all under the Vosges umbrella." In 2011, she kicked off the project in Belize, planting fields of cocoa bean varietals and opening a production facility. Next up are micro bean-to-bar production plants in cities around the United States, where people can tour a factory as part of their chocolate tasting experience.

Vosges is also evolving with the changing perceptions and experience of luxury. In a world of flash sales, outlet deals, and cheap-chic collaborations, does "luxury" even exist anymore? Katrina believes it does, and never wants to put the Vosges name on a lesser product lest it hurt the brand's identity. But at the same time, there *is* a strong market for products at a lower (but still moderate) price point. So in 2012, Katrina launched Vosges's "younger sister" brand, Wild Ophelia, as a next-generation candy bar. "They're related, but if Vosges is couture, Wild Ophelia is ready to wear—it's young, independent, and purely American, and we can sell it for about half the price of Vosges," she says. Unlike Vosges, Wild Ophelia bars—flavors include beef jerky, smokehouse BBQ potato chips, and Southern hibiscus peach—are sold at places like Target and Walgreens. And without the cost of high-end boutiques, lush packaging and catalogs, and exotic ingredients, Katrina can charge less. And the larger market gives her additional economies of scale. So far, both brands seem to be growing in tandem in their distinct markets: While her flagship Vosges brand is completely sustainable, this offshoot opens up a whole new world for Katrina to play in, while still applying some of the lessons she's learned in luxury marketing.

In 2001, Katrina was thrilled with Vosges's first $150,000 of profits. A short decade later, in 2012, Vosges had estimated revenues of $30 million a year. And they'd gone from having twelve employees in 2001 to well over a hundred today. But for Katrina, the best part is that it's now part of her purpose to travel the world through food. Everywhere she journeys, alone or with her husband and children, is an opportunity to experience new tastes and new cultures, which ultimately weave their way into her confections. Today, people travel the world through her chocolates—and her chocolates most definitely travel the world.

TAKE AWAY

- **To create a sense of luxury and worth, tell a story.** Take a beautiful photo, then write or talk about where and how the item was made and the special, precise details. The goal is to connect customers to the product so they see the value in the price tag. That luxury story should also come through in the logo, packaging, and retail locations.

- **Purposefully position your brand.** For example, Katrina wanted to position Vosges the way couture fashion companies did: as a brand that sold limited-edition items in high-end department stores and boutiques. Instead of pursuing mass-market distribution, use things like specialty stores, e-commerce, and partnerships with other luxury brands to gain awareness and sales channels.

- **Expand the luxury concept carefully.** Katrina has twice added new lines to her original fancy truffle/boutique concept—first with Vosges chocolate bars, sold at places like Whole Foods, and then with Wild Ophelia bars, which are available at locations like Walgreens. Each time, she considered how it would affect the flagship brand; Vosges bars were on target, but the lower-priced Wild Ophelia would debut under a different label. Expanding into new markets is always good, but make sure to keep your luxury identity safe.

MORE INSIDER ADVICE

Tips from a Food Cart Owner, Blogger, Caterer, and Food Market Organizer

Insider Advice from . . . the Food Cart Owner

Kir Jensen, owner of the Sugar Cube, a food cart in Portland, Oregon

After working in fine-dining kitchens for years, pastry chef Kir was ready to do her own thing, but she didn't have the capital required to open a bakery. Instead, she bought a food cart and turned it into a tiny, polished eight- by fourteen-foot mobile kitchen. Now Kir sells her treats, like chocolate caramel potato chip cupcakes and Guinness-ginger cake, from a parking lot in downtown Portland. Here, she shares what she's learned:

1. Trucks and carts are great for focusing on a niche area—say, desserts, hand-roasted coffee, or pulled pork. Which one should you choose? Portland has a thriving cart scene, and there are places where we can park for a long time. On the other hand, food trucks are more mobile and can go wherever there's a crowd, like a street fair or sports game. And social media means customers always know where their favorite truck is.

2. Carts don't fly under the radar: I still have to comply with the same licensing requirements and health regulations as restaurants.

3. I'm at the mercy of the elements: weather and vandalism become big issues. Sunny days mean good foot traffic and sales, but people don't stop by a food cart in cold, rainy weather. Have a buffer—six months of living expenses—to get through the winter months. And I have to be prepared for crime and vandalism because my cart is outside each night with very little to protect it.

4. A small space forces you to be efficient, and that's a good thing! After I make a batch of something, I have to clean up completely before making the next item. And small batches mean customers usually get a treat straight out of the oven, which they love.

Insider Advice from . . . the Food Blogger

Adam Roberts, *The Amateur Gourmet* (AmateurGourmet.com)

1. There's a big difference between blogging as a hobby and blogging as a business. Most successful bloggers I know started writing from an authentic place for various reasons—rarely was it to earn money—and then it grew into something. Ultimately, success comes when people connect to you and your voice.

2. If you want to make money from your blog, you need to be practical from the beginning. You'll need a great concept (such as the

Julie/Julia Project) and a unique point of view. Then you have to purposefully write posts that generate traffic. Be honest with yourself; if no one is commenting on or coming to your blog after a few months of regular posting, you might need to rethink your initial concept.

3. There are a few types of posts that will get you traffic and attention: the stunningly beautiful recipe, the crazy idea, and the emotionally forthcoming story. Beautiful recipes are hard to win on; there are thousands of blog posts with chili recipes, for example, and to get real traffic you would need to have one of the best. But an attention-grabbing, crazy chili recipe—say, how to make chili in a Ziploc bag—can get people to click. For example, I got my big break when I made a Janet Jackson cupcake after the 2004 Super Bowl debacle. The day before, I had twenty hits. Then I came home and found I'd received 80,000 hits in just a few hours. A more gradual, but very effective, way to gain traffic is with emotionally forthcoming posts. Molly Wizenberg of *Orangette* is a great example; she puts her personal struggles out there and connects with her readers on a deeper level.

4. Your blog doesn't have to be the end game. The food blogging community is huge, and incredibly supportive. Maybe your blog doesn't bring in a lot of money, but when you move on to another food project—a restaurant or selling packaged baked goods—all of those blog friends will support you.

Insider Advice from . . . the Celebrity Caterer

Peter Callahan, owner of Peter Callahan Catering, which caters events for A-listers like Martha Stewart, Vera Wang, Kelly Ripa, and Al Gore

1. Be known for a specific concept. Think about how many caterers are out there—they can all look alike! If you're in that vein, you really need to build out your sales team and your marketing materials to get jobs. Instead, look around. If someone else is doing it, you don't want to; differentiate yourself. For example, I do whimsical, small bites that make people smile—cracker "spoons" topped with caviar, shrimp "lollipops," and tiny burgers. Find a special type of food to focus on, and you'll automatically stand out from the crowd.

2. Be as unbusiness-like as possible. It might sound counterintuitive, but we're doing parties here, not writing up wills or performing surgery! Parties are supposed to be fun! So make it about fun and take a really lighthearted approach. Every time you interact with a client, try to be bright, funny, and happy.

3. When people ask for a proposal, suggest meeting to talk instead. This isn't about black ink on white paper, it's about food and relationships! I've never gotten a job from a proposal, but I've gotten lots of jobs from meeting people. And when you meet a potential client, be yourself.

4. Everything is in the planning, but then you have to go with the flow. There will always be curveballs during an event—more or

fewer guests than you planned on, an unannounced toast, pictures that run long. No matter what happens, you just have to be that calm, smiling person. It helps if that's who you are naturally on the inside!

Insider Advice from . . . the Food Market Founder

Eric Demby, cofounder of the popular Brooklyn food fair Smorgasburg

1. Scout far and wide for vendors. When we were first starting the precursor to Smorgasburg, the Brooklyn Flea Market, in 2008—and had zero exposure or name recognition—I looked everywhere for potential vendors. For example, I saw a small blurb in the *New York Times* on two women making homemade ricotta; I reached out, met one for drinks, and they ended up being one of our first vendors. Or I knew that a group of Mexican vendors who sold at area baseball fields were looking for a new home, so I invited them to come under our umbrella. That way, when we opened we had people doing interesting things and it garnered lots of press.

2. Talk to the health department first thing. I attribute a big part of our success to simply visiting the city health department and asking what, exactly, we'd need to do to be compliant. They really appreciated us asking upfront because a lot of food people don't. And it was the start of a good relationship: After several years of working with the department, they agreed to increase the time frame of the required vendor permit from two weeks to

one year. We also found that each tent needs to have someone on site who is certified in food safety and any food that's not made on site has to be made in a commercial kitchen.

3. Curate the right mix. Today, we get about fifteen applications a week from new vendors and can accept less than one of those. So we're looking at a variety of factors, and delicious food is just the baseline requirement. We want an interesting personal narrative and a unique product (a best-ever cheeseburger doesn't cut it); global flavors are always a plus.

4. Selling at a food fair is a doable business model. I never would have guessed that people would create their business with Smorgasburg in mind. It's not a stepping-stone to a restaurant or packaged product anymore, it's the end game. But it works!

ACKNOWLEDGMENTS

It's true, what they say: it takes a village to write a book. To the many, many people who made *Cooking Up a Business* a reality, I offer my deepest thanks.

To Kari Stuart, my agent at ICM, who deserves pages and pages of praise. Thank you for taking a chance on this book—and me—and shaping it into what it is today, and for your never-ending support, enthusiasm, and friendship.

To my editors (and aspiring food entrepreneurs!) at Perigee: Maria Gagliano, who said yes to this book, and Jeanette Shaw, who gracefully turned a manuscript into this book. And to designer Sara Wood, for creating a cover I love. Finally, a thousand thanks go to Grace Gavilanes, my assistant extraordinaire, for her capable help and smart insights.

And my deepest respect goes to the great magazine editors who have taught me how to interview, write, edit, and most of all, tell great stories: Chandra Turner, Michelle Shih, Celia Barbour, Susan Schulz Wuornos, Sally Abbey, Diane Dragan, and Courtenay Smith.

My deepest, heartfelt gratitude goes to my wonderful colleagues, friends, and family who read chapters and offered their wise and insightful feedback: Lynn Andriani, Sara Barbour, Celia Barbour,

Kevin Curry, Joan Draper, Cara Eisenpress, Grace Gavilanes, Brooke Glassberg, Lorne Hofstetter, Dana Hofstetter, Phoebe Lapine, Elizabeth Mount, Kathleen Mount, Steven Mount, Martha Odell, Mariko O'Neill, Kate Rockwood, Gemma Rogers, Michelle Shih, Stacey Goers, Sara Spiedel, Jessica Strul, Kari Stuart, Tammy Tibbetts, Devin Tomb, Elizabeth Wood, and Cassandra Zink.

And I started off this book with a dedication to four people who truly made this book happen, and they deserve yet another round of thanks: cheers to Steve, Kathleen, Tammy, and Lorne.

And finally, my resounding thanks goes to the entrepreneurs and experts who gave so freely of their time and expertise, and as much of a thank you to their PR teams and assistants who helped me arrange countless interviews and logistics. It's been my greatest pleasure to share your inspiring stories.

INDEX

Page numbers in *italics* indicate figures or photographs.

ABOUT THE AUTHOR

Shea Roggio

A former food editor at *O, the Oprah Magazine* and *Reader's Digest*, **Rachel Mount Hofstetter** is now founder in chief at *guesterly* magazine. She received a degree in economics from Miami University and lives in New York City with her husband, Lorne. Find her on Twitter @rachelhoffy.